# Matilda
## *Lady* of *Hay*

# Matilda
*Lady of Hay*

*The Life and Legends of Matilda de Braose*

PETER FORD

LOGASTON PRESS 🍍

FRONT COVER: Period photograph of Hay Castle from the north. When the impressive gateway was built *c*.1200, the arches in the ancient gatehouse were sealed up and it was converted into the keep. The windows were added during subsequent rebuilding work. Lady in twelfth-century costume from an illustration by Percy Anderson in *Costumes Fanciful, Historical and Theatrical* (Macmillan & Co., 1906)

FRONTISPIECE: Aerial view of Hay Castle from the south (*photograph © Paul R. Davis*)

First published in 2018 (three impressions, Amazon paperback).
This edition published in 2021 by Logaston Press,
The Holme, Church Road, Eardisley HR3 6NJ, UK
www.logastonpress.co.uk
An imprint of Fircone Books Ltd.

ISBN 978-1-910839-43-0

Designed and typeset by Richard Wheeler in 10 on 14.5 Minion
Cover design by Richard Wheeler.

Printed and bound in Wales.

Logaston Press is committed to a sustainable future for our business, our readers and our planet. This book is made from paper certified by the Forest Stewardship Council.

British Library Catalogue in Publishing Data.
A CIP catalogue record for this book is available from the British Library.

# CONTENTS

*To Hay Castle,*

*Matilda was one of your original builders but the centuries have not been kind to you. Thankfully you are now re-emerging for a new life in fine form, thanks to the work of the Hay Castle Trust.*

*To Angela,*

*Your help and support made this book possible.*

## ACKNOWLEDGEMENTS

All history of Hay builds on the work of Geoffrey Fairs, but I would like to acknowledge the support of the members of the Hay History Group, whose aim it is to continue to record the history of Hay for future generations. Grateful thanks to Philip Hume, for kindly reading the manuscript and suggesting a number of amendments, and for permission to use the Marcher lordships map on p. 5. Also, to Richard and Su Wheeler of Logaston Press for their work on this edition.

In particular I owe a debt of gratitude to Mari Fforde for introducing me to Matilda, and for her enthusiasm for all things Hay.

# PREFACE

Matilda Lady of Haya, Haia, La Haie, Hale, Haye has been a legendary figure in Brecknockshire and Radnorshire for centuries. She figured strongly in the destiny of her husband William III de Braose, and also that of King John.

I became fascinated with the myths and legends surrounding Matilda on moving to Hay-on-Wye in 2015. After becoming secretary of the local history group, I became a guide at Hay Castle, and so was able to see Matilda's buildings at first hand – the keep, the gateway and the walls. Walking in Matilda's footsteps increased my interest and led me to research everything I could about this fascinating woman.

Stories tell of how Matilda led her own army against the Welsh in support of her husband William – the 'Ogre of Abergavenny' – and how, later, she was ruthlessly hunted, captured and starved to death by a vindictive King John; whilst legends developed that she built Hay Castle in one night.

Were her outspoken comments about King John murdering his nephew really the cause of her outlawing? Why is she credited with witch-like powers, such as being able to throw a three-ton stone cross over the River Wye? Is her legacy discernible in the Magna Carta?

Over the past 30 years, Matilda has become better known through the publication of the best selling novel *The Lady of Hay* by Barbara Erskine. But that is fiction. Just who was the real Matilda de Braose?

My intention in this book is to introduce the story of Matilda to a wider audience. By describing the woman in the context of her time and exploring the legends, I hope to clarify, or at least open a debate on, how they may have arisen.

Almost all that we know about Matilda comes from the writings of three chroniclers: Gerald of Wales, the so-called Anonymous of Bethune and Matthew Paris; however, Matilda also figures in the surviving contemporary government records of the reign of King John. Later references by antiquarians Theophilus Jones and John Leland, record local legends about her mythical status among the Welsh, under the names of Moll or Maud Walbee or Walbec.

To add to the challenge of the research, the names Maud and Matilda were very common in the Middle Ages and were often used interchangeably. Other variations found in medieval documents are 'Mathilde' and 'Mahalt'. To avoid confusion 'Matilda' is used throughout this book.

Hay Castle mansion in its heyday, with the original castle keep almost smothered by ivy, and the gateway completely hidden by vegetation

# INTRODUCTION

Matilda was born nearly 100 years after William the Conqueror invaded England; however in order to explain Matilda's story we need to understand how William organised control of the border between England and Wales.

In reality, William's defeat of the Saxon King Harold at the Battle of Hastings in 1066 marked only the beginning of the Norman Conquest of England. William was compelled to campaign, and put down, multiple insurrections until 1074–5, when England was finally subjugated. Whilst needing to bring England under his control, William's approach to Wales would be quite different.

Historically, the English-Welsh border had been fluid for centuries. From the time of the Romans' withdrawal from Britain in the fifth century, the border fluctuated depending on the power and ambitions of the princes of Wales against that of the kings of Mercia. When the princes were in the ascendancy the border moved eastwards and when the Mercian kings were strong it moved westwards. Any attempts to create a meaningful border, such as the construction of Offa's Dyke in the eighth century, ultimately proved futile.

Traditionally, the border between Wales and England had been marked by the River Severn, according to Gerald of Wales, writing at the end of the twelfth century. However, he acknowledged that this was changing, and by c.1200 it was more accurately demarcated by the Rivers Wye and Dee. Indeed, access to the remoter lowlands of the border region was often by water along the rivers.

The Anglo-Saxons referred to the area as a *mearc* – a border region. Similarly, it had become known to the Welsh as the *Wallenses* – literally 'the borders'. Both terms denoted a region in which borders could fluctuate, with similar areas existing on the English-Scottish borders and the borders of Normandy.

The March between England and Wales could be an area of incursion and violence from both sides. The Welsh could raid, burn settlements and quickly take cattle, before returning to the safety of the uplands. The rural population was sparse, as evidenced by the Domesday Book. It describes Clifford, a few miles from Hay, as wasteland due to the border warfare that had occurred 20 to 30 years earlier, although it is known that a few inhabitants lived in the area.

It appears that in the middle of the eleventh century, the concept of the Welsh March on the English-Welsh border was similar to that which people take it to mean these days – namely, the lands of western Shropshire and Herefordshire that cross into eastern Powys. Over the next 200 years, however, under the Anglo-Normans, the Welsh March changed, from being a border region, to a separate and distinct region that lay between England and Wales, politically part of neither, and defined by the nearly 50 Marcher lordships that were created during that period. Its geographical extent grew to encompass lands that are now parts of Cheshire, Worcestershire and Gloucestershire (as well as Shropshire and Herefordshire), part of Flintshire, all of Denbighshire, Powys (Montgomeryshire, Radnorshire and Brecknockshire), Monmouthshire and south Wales all the way across to Pembrokeshire.

As a consequence, the lands of the Welsh princes from Anglesey and Snowdonia in the north to Ceredigion in the west became known as 'Wales proper' or *Pura Wallia*, and the frontier lands of the Anglo-Norman March of Wales in the south and east as *Marchia Wallie*. Often the new Norman lordships were based on the traditional Welsh administrative divisions of cantrefs and commotes. Although settlers were often brought in from England (and further afield), particularly on the lands surrounding castles, the native Welsh remained, albeit often pushed back into the more marginal land of the uplands. In many areas this came to be formalised into the 'Englishries' and the 'Welshries' within a lordship.

William the Conqueror's approach to Wales, therefore, was quite different to the experience in England. Conquest of Wales was unnecessary as his Anglo-Saxon predecessors, as the kings of the English, had established a tradition of overlordship of the Welsh princes. William was also aware that in addition, any attempt at conquest would be time-consuming and expensive as the mountains provided both a secure refuge and a fragmented polity that was difficult to defeat.

Had he attempted an invasion, William faced the prospect of a protracted guerrilla war, for which the Norman fighting machine was not equipped. A century later, Prince John found this out when he invaded Ireland in 1185. The heavy armour and high saddles of the *destriers*, the war horses, made mounting and dismounting slow and difficult. Unfortunately, this was essential in a war against guerrilla forces.

William would also have had to face the Welsh longbow. This was a formidable weapon. Gerald of Wales notes that it was made from a dwarf elm tree and was thick and powerful.[1] Shorter than the English longbow, its arrows did not fly as far but flew very level and straight. Reputedly, it was capable of killing a horse after first going through a man's thigh encased in armour, and then the saddle. Modern archers have tested wych elm bows and found they are only slightly inferior to those made of yew.

Fighting against such a weapon, in the relentless rain, tangled woods and impassable bogs of Wales, meant that gaining a significant victory would be nigh on impossible, and casualties would be high. An example of this occurred after the Welsh uprising, begun in 1094 to reclaim their lands that had been lost to the Anglo-Normans. After earlier incursions by William fitz Osbern, the seizure of Brycheiniog by Bernard de Neufmarché in 1093 had launched Norman advances across all of central and southern Wales. Within a year, though, much had been reclaimed by the Welsh.

In 1096, an Anglo-Norman force moved into Gwent but met with no success. Returning empty-handed, they were defeated by the men of Gwent at Kellitravant (Celi Carnant). In the same year, when the Normans advanced for a second time, they built a series of timber and earth motte and bailey castles as strongholds as they went along.

Despite this, they were ambushed at Aberllech[2] and driven off by a force from Brecknockshire under the Welsh princes Gruffudd and Ifor, the sons of Idnerth ap Cadwgan.[3] The exact site of the battle is uncertain, but it was on the borders of the Brecon Beacons near Abercraf, deep in Wales.

## The Marcher lords

With foresight, William adopted an alternative strategy. To hold these lands, and keep the indigenous Welsh in check, he appointed particularly strong, loyal knights along the border.

William created the earldoms of Chester, Shrewsbury and Hereford. The knights he chose were, respectively, Hugh d'Avranches, Roger of Montgomery and William fitz Osbern. They were among his strongest and most ruthless followers, veterans of the invasion, or in fitz Osbern's case his deputy in England. William gave them extensive powers to secure their earldoms, and possibly an understanding that they could encroach into disputed lands in Wales.

By Matilda's time, Ranulf de Blondeville was the 6th earl of Chester. He was stepfather to Prince Arthur of Brittany (of whom more later). However, both the earldoms of Hereford and Shrewsbury had lapsed (in 1075 and 1102 respectively) with the barons in the former earldoms, such as de Lacy, de Braose and Mortimer, becoming now powerful tenants-in-chief of the Crown. Over time, barons such as these established their lands as Marcher lordships.

Although the Marcher lords acquired unique powers, they remained tenants-in-chief of the Crown. Consequently, whilst in normal circumstances the lordships passed down through families, in the event of (failed) rebellion or there being no heir at all, the lordship became the property of the king to be allocated elsewhere. Female inheritance meant that the lordship passed to the family of her husband. Some Normans intermarried with the native Welsh, creating new alliances and altering the dynamics of the political scene.

Over the century or so after the Conquest the Norman barons built up their empires. Wisely, the reigning monarchs ensured that their various estates were distributed all over the country. The de Clares at

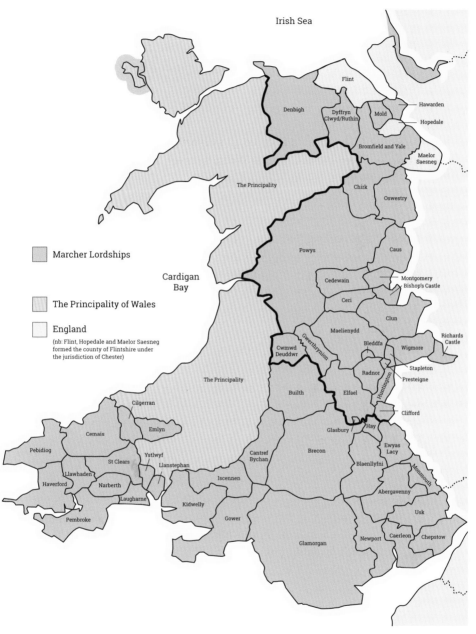

The Marcher lordships and the Principality of Wales after 1284 (© *Jason Appleby*)

one time were lords of Pembroke and Striguil, earls of Gloucester and Hertford, and also held estates in Ireland. Decentralising their estates in this way meant that however powerful a baron became he had no central base from which to challenge the reigning king.

During the 200 years after 1066, the Marcher lordships came into being partly through the conquest of new territories in Wales, partly through powerful barons withdrawing their border lordships from English jurisdiction into the March, and partly through new ones being created by Edward I in 1277–83. Over this period, the Marcher lords were allowed to claim unique powers derived from those given to the first earls, and also those that had been exercised by Welsh princes in the conquered lands. Many of these powers were normally reserved for the king. They were referred to as 'lords royal', able to run almost sovereign states with exemption from taxes, rights to grant charters, to hold their own courts, create their own private armies and build castles. All this they could do without obtaining the king's permission which other lords in England were obliged to seek. They were even allowed to make war on each other.

Despite this independence they all ultimately owed allegiance to the king. The Norman system of feudal loyalty meant lords held their lands from the king in return for fighting service. Each lord then gave land to a number of his knights, who owed service to the lord, and through him the king. They in turn had tenants who owed allegiance through the knight to the lord, and ultimately the king.

This feudal system meant lords were able to call upon their knights and raise an army at will. With this they could support the king, attack the Welsh or defend themselves from other lords.

The Anglo-Normans were notorious for their seizure of additional land at every opportunity. Being able to raise an army facilitated this. It was not long before the Marcher lords obtained control of the borders across to mid-Wales and all of south Wales as far as Pembroke. As the area of land increased so did the number of lords, and in time there were nearly 50 Marcher lordships (*see map on p. 5*).

The upland areas of mid- and north Wales were another matter. This was the realm of the Welsh princes and only the king was powerful enough to challenge them on their home ground. King John had to raise a large army in 1211 to quell the rebellion of Llywelyn ab Iorwerth, Llywelyn the Great, who was ruler of Gwynedd in the north of Wales.

Edward I's conquest of Wales in 1282–83 ended the rule of the native Welsh princes in the lands of *Pura Wallia* in the north and the west. Instead, these lands became the Principality of Wales administered by the representatives of the English Crown. The Edwardian settlement also recognised the existence of the nearly 50 Marcher lordships as an area that lay between England and Wales, not fully part of either country.

## The Laws of the March

Clause 56 of the Magna Carta of 1215 covered disputes over land or liberties taken from Welshmen in the general area of the March. If the tenement was in England it was covered by the Laws of England; if in Wales by the Laws of Wales; but in the March by the Laws of the March.

These Marcher laws were never officially established, and were never written down or codified. They existed in memory and tradition, and evolved over time from the laws of the Welsh and English common law.

The Welsh system of law was developed from Cyfraith Hywel, 'the law of Hywel', whose development is traditionally ascribed to King Hywel ap Cadell, who died in 950. It was a compensation-based written system, of which nearly 40 manuscripts survive.[4] The focus of the law was mutual responsibility, and it continued to evolve for four centuries.

As described above, the almost regal powers of the Marcher lords included the right to establish their own courts which administered their own laws. Initially, these were all based on English law but over time the Marcher lords found it expedient to interpret and adopt aspects of Welsh law. This flexibility was particularly apparent where land was involved, and over time a private system of jurisprudence started to evolve.[5]

In 1297 Edmund Mortimer granted his men in Maelienydd trial before a jury of 12 men, and John fitz Reginald did the same two years later for the men of Talgarth to the south. A particularly impressive charter by William vii de Braose granted and confirmed all existing rights and liberties to the men of Gower in 1306.

The Kidwelly Charters of 1356 granted by Henry, duke of Lancaster, went further and formally incorporated aspects of the law of Hywel Dŵr. By 1391 the name of the king was removed from legal documents in the north-east March and replaced by the earl of Arundel's name as the lord of the area. The other major influence was the legal judgements recorded in the court rolls, the royal decisions in cases involving the Marcher lords. The reigning monarchs would adhere to English common law when dealing with them, and also to cases referred on appeal to the English legal system.[6]

All the evidence of how this evolved is fragmentary, and the Marcher laws were never written down, but they are evidenced by the lords' use of their autonomous powers. The Laws of the March enabled them to maintain a degree of independence from the Crown, and confirmed individual lords' judicial independence from one another.

Over the centuries, concerns grew that the existence of around 50 separate jurisdictions across the Principality of Wales and the Marcher lordships was a significant factor in the increasing breakdown of law and order in Wales and the Marches. In 1473, when Edward iv sent his three-year-old son, Prince Edward, the Prince of Wales, to live in Ludlow, he created a council to administer, on behalf of the young prince, his lands of the Principality and those Marcher lordships granted to him (by this time, many of the Marcher lordships now belonged to the Crown). Although initially a household council to administer the Principality and the young prince's Marcher lordships, Edward iv and subsequent kings gradually increased its powers. It became responsible for general law and order and also a court of appeal for all the Marcher lordships and the border counties of Cheshire, Shropshire, Herefordshire and Worcestershire, and for some cases a court of first instance.

The Laws in Wales Acts of 1536 and 1542 abolished the Principality and also the powers of the Marcher lords, with the lordships incorporated into the administration of the new counties of Wales, or the existing border counties of England. For the first time Wales was governed in a similar way to England, with a structure of justices, courts and sessions. The Council in the Marches of Wales was formally established with enhanced powers, though it too was abolished in 1689.

## Marcher Castles

William the Conqueror's 'secret weapon' in his conquest of England in 1066 was the motte and bailey castle. This consisted of a wooden tower on an earth mound, the motte, surrounded by a wooden fence or palisade, the bailey. These were relatively cheap and quick to build and appeared all over the country. Nowhere did they become more abundant than on the English-Welsh border.

In the early days after the Conquest, the Marcher lords constructed a large number of these fortifications. They were essential strongholds from which to control land in the new areas taken from the Welsh. As time went by, the lords consolidated their hold by rebuilding a number of these temporary structures into permanent stone castles (although a few castles – for example Chepstow and Ludlow – were built in stone from the outset).

Clifford Castle is an example of this. In the first Norman incursion into Wales along the Wye Valley, William fitz Osbern, earl of Hereford, advanced as far as Hay. Here he defeated a Welsh army. To secure his line of advance he built a motte and bailey castle on a cliff overlooking a ford of the river at Clifford, five miles from Hay. It was subsequently rebuilt in stone.

Subsequently, Bernard de Neufmarché continued the advance from Hay, getting as far as Brecknock in 1088. Bernard built a castle at Brecknock, but to confirm his hold on the area he gave one of his knights, Sir Philip Walwyn, permission to build a motte and bailey castle at Hay.

The remains of the motte are still visible on the natural defensive position in the crook of land between the River Wye and the Login Brook. Shortly afterwards, St Mary's Church was built nearby. The castle was a temporary stronghold and the motte was never rebuilt in stone. When the town walls were built 150 years later, this area was not included as the focus of the town had shifted further east.

The remains of the mound (known locally as the Tump) from the original motte and bailey castle thought to have been built by Sir Philip Walwyn in c.1088, on the western edge of Hay (*photograph © Paul R. Davis*)

The volatility of the English-Welsh border region can be seen in the highest concentration of motte and bailey castles found anywhere in the country. Around Hay, other similar castles were built at Mouse Castle, Cusop, Painscastle and Llanthomas near Llanigon, as well as two at Clyro. To maintain a firm hold on the area, the ones at Clyro, Cusop and Painscastle were later rebuilt in stone.

In Hay, a new stone castle emerged in what became the centre of the town, built on a stronger defensive site.

# CHAPTER 1

# William III de Braose and Matilda

MATILDA's husband, William III de Braose was one of the most powerful barons in the country at the time of King John. He held extensive estates throughout England and Wales, and was a key supporter of first King Richard I and then King John.

William's Norman lineage dated back to before the time of the Conquest, as his family held estates at Briouze in north-west France. This gave rise to a multitude of family names – including Briouze, Brewose, Breuse, Brewes, Brehuse and, in Latin, de Briousa. Most importantly for the family fortunes, William's great-grandfather was in Duke William's army when he left Normandy and invaded England in 1066.

After William became the Conqueror by defeating Harold at Hastings, he was concerned that the south coast represented a potential weakness to his new kingdom. If he could invade, so could others. The newly-crowned King William sought to protect the south coast by granting land there to the most dependable knights who had accompanied him across from Normandy.

One of these, William I de Braose, was made 1st lord of Bramber in Sussex,[1] as well as being given estates around Wareham and Purbeck in Dorset. This was ironic given subsequent events.[2] In turn, his son Philip, and then his grandson William II, succeeded to the lordship.[3]

William II was a staunch supporter of King Henry II, as was his brother Philip, and they both acquired land and power during his reign. In Henry's time of crisis in 1173, when Scotland invaded and his sons rebelled, William II was made sheriff of Hereford.

At the end of the eleventh century, William I or his son, Philip, had been granted the Marcher lordship of Radnor to the east of Hay, and had conquered Builth to the west. When William II's wife Bertha, the daughter of Miles of Gloucester, earl of Hereford, inherited the Marcher lordships of Abergavenny and Brecknock, this resulted in William II becoming the most powerful baron in the central Marches and brought Hay (a sub-lordship of Brecknock) into their control. Bertha's mother was Sybil, daughter of Bernard de Neufmarché, which was again an important lineage as Bernard's grandfather was also one of the knights who came over at the Conquest.

## William III de Braose

William II de Braose died in c.1190–92 leaving his son William III to inherit and manage the large estates he had built up. Not only did William III become the 4th Lord Bramber, he was also the sheriff of Hereford from 1192–99. Additionally, through his mother's great-grandfather Bernard de Neufmarché, he became 7th baron of Abergavenny, lord of Brecknock, as well as claiming the lordships of Radnor and Builth.

The date of birth of William III is uncertain, being sometime between 1144 and 1153 (with good evidence for 24 December 1153 from some sources). He is sometimes referred to by his French forename, Guillaume. William was distantly related to his wife-to-be Matilda, as the two ancestral lines of Bernard de Neufmarché and Matilda's father Bernard de Saint-Valery were descended from the sons of the first Bernard de Saint-Valery who was born about 947.

As well as being a large landholder, William was an influential supporter of the Crown. He accompanied Richard I to France and was with him when he was killed at Chalus in 1199. When his younger brother John claimed the throne, William transferred his allegiance to him. William was pivotal in persuading the other barons to accept John as king.[4] As a result, a degree of trust developed between both men, and William became an integral part of John's inner circle and decision-making.

As a reward for this loyalty, William was given extensive lands by John in the early part of his reign, as evidenced in the official Pipe Rolls, Book of Fees and Red Book of the Exchequer. This was not altogether

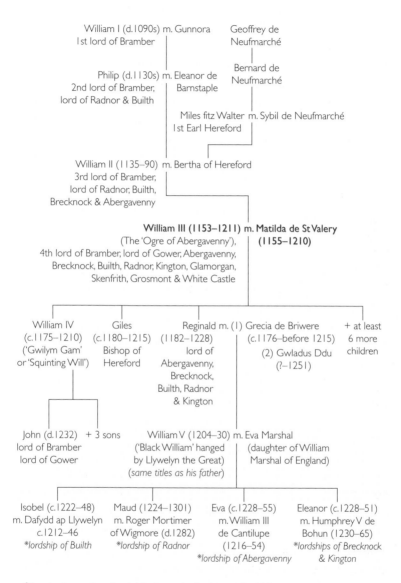

William I (d.1090s) m. Gunnora
1st lord of Bramber

Geoffrey de
Neufmarché

Philip (d.1130s) m. Eleanor de
2nd lord of Bramber,    Barnstaple
lord of Radnor & Builth

Bernard de
Neufmarché

Miles fitz Walter m. Sybil de Neufmarché
1st Earl Hereford

William II (1135–90) m. Bertha of Hereford
3rd lord of Bramber,
lord of Radnor, Builth,
Brecknock & Abergavenny

**William III (1153–1211) m. Matilda de St Valery**
(The 'Ogre of Abergavenny'),     (1155–1210)
4th lord of Bramber, lord of Gower, Abergavenny,
Brecknock, Builth, Radnor, Kington, Glamorgan,
Skenfrith, Grosmont & White Castle

William IV
(c.1175–1210)
('Gwilym Gam'
or 'Squinting Will')

Giles
(c.1180–1215)
Bishop of
Hereford

Reginald m. (1) Grecia de Briwere
(1182–1228)    (c.1176–before 1215)
lord of
Abergavenny,     (2) Gwladus Ddu
Brecknock,        (?–1251)
Builth, Radnor
& Kington

+ at least
6 more
children

John (d.1232) + 3 sons
lord of Bramber
lord of Gower

William V (1204–30) m. Eva Marshal
('Black William' hanged     (daughter of William
by Llywelyn the Great)      Marshal of England)
(same titles as his father)

Isobel (c.1222–48)
m. Dafydd ap Llywelyn
c.1212–46
*lordship of Builth

Maud (1224–1301)
m. Roger Mortimer
of Wigmore (d.1282)
*lordship of Radnor

Eva (c.1228–55)
m. William III
de Cantilupe
(1216–54)
*lordship of Abergavenny

Eleanor (c.1228–51)
m. Humphrey V de
Bohun (1230–65)
*lordships of Brecknock
& Kington

*denotes the portion of each inheritance the daughter took with her

A select de Braose family tree

altruistic as John was adept at balancing threats from dissident lords
with those in whom he had the utmost faith and trust. Consequently,
giving William land in Ireland and along the Welsh border helped to
neutralise threats to John's reign from other barons in those areas.

William was a tough warrior, fearless and ruthless when needed.[5]
In time he increased his lands across the whole of the lower half of
England and Wales. In the south these included parts of Sussex, Devon
and Wiltshire. As well as land in Shropshire and Herefordshire, he
held estates in Gloucestershire at Tetbury and Hampnett, which came
to him on his marriage to Matilda.

In addition to the Marcher lordships of his inheritance – Brecknock
(including Hay), Abergavenny, Radnor and Builth – William went on to
seize control of the Welsh cantref of Elfael, which included Painscastle,
and was granted Kington, the castles of Skenfrith, Grosmont and White
Castle, and the lordship of Gower in south Wales, by the king. In time,
William ended up with a block of land from south Shropshire to the
Gower Peninsular and out to Pembrokeshire.

Overseas, in addition to his inherited family estates at Briouze in
Normandy, William was later made lord of Limerick and Munster in
Ireland by John. With all these estates, William was arguably the most
important land-owning baron in the country.

The life of a Marcher lord typically involved a great deal of campaigning. In addition to accompanying John on campaign in France,
much of William's time was spent around Brecknock and mid-Wales.
These were turbulent times and there were constant skirmishes and
raids between the Welsh and the Anglo-Normans – with the Welsh
princes often forming alliances with and against the Norman Marcher
lords, to reclaim their lands.

For all William's reputation for bluff warrior ruthlessness, he also
appears to have been able to demonstrate guile and astuteness, particularly when it came to legal matters. Herbert fitz Herbert unsuccessfully
claimed one third of Brecknockshire from William in 1199. Herbert's
son Peter pursued the claim in 1206, but William used the legal device
of *essoin* in order to delay the case for over a year, claiming illness.
Peter eventually gained control of this area after the fall of William.

In another case, also in 1206, William simply failed to turn up in court to answer a summons in Surrey.[6]

William also knew how to use the full power of the law. In one case he paid 300 cows, 30 bulls and 10 horses in order to submit a plea to the courts.[7] By using his position as a close confidant of the king, he was able to play the legal system to his advantage.

The royal charters confirm that he had a key role in the royal court. William witnessed more royal charters than any other layman. It may be this access to the workings of court, and events such as the disappearance of Arthur of Brittany,[8] that ultimately gave rise to John's enmity and led to William and Matilda's downfall. John exerted political power through cracking down on debt, and he used the excuse that William owed him money to destroy his loyal baron.

William had a reputation for vacillation when it came to paying his debts. He had owed large sums of money to both King Henry and King Richard, which John wrote off at the start of his reign.[9] Similarly, William may have believed that as a royal favourite he would never be expected to fulfil his debts to John. However, when John rewarded his barons with gifts of castles, lordships or estates he expected them to pay for them. Those in the king's favour might be allowed to postpone the debt – at least until they fell out with the king – but not to pay was to invite the king's wrath.[10]

William had agreed to pay John 5,000 marks for the lordship of Munster, at 500 marks a year, and further money for the honour of Limerick, when he received them from John in 1201/2. On the face of it William should have been rich enough to pay his debts.

One scholar, Sidney Painter,[11] has calculated that at the height of William's power he had an income of between £800 and £1,000 per annum. This was a phenomenal sum in a time when labourers typically earned 1d a day, and you could live comfortably on £10 a year. William's estates included some 16 castles, and 852 knights owed allegiance through him to the king.

By 1210, at the time of John's pursuit of William in Ireland, William was out of favour. John justified his action by claiming that William had not paid a single mark for his 'gifts' and that William owed him

40,000 marks for past 'favours'. While this was not strictly true as William had paid 700 marks by 1207[12] it suited John to claim otherwise.

## Matilda de Saint-Valery

Matilda was born Maud de Saint-Valery-en-Caux. She came from the little coastal town of this name in Seine-Maritime, Haute-Normandie, France, 20 miles west of Dieppe. The settlement was founded in the 7th century by Saint Waleric and became a busy port during the Middle Ages. The town is notable as the point where William the Conqueror assembled his fleet and waited out a storm, before sailing the Channel, intent on his conquest of England.[13]

Matilda was the daughter of Bernard IV, Seigneur de Saint-Valery and his first wife Matilda Isleworth. The family had lived at Saint-Valery-en-Caux since the tenth century and had strong Norman lineage. Matilda's great-great-grandfather Bernard II was one of the knights with William at the Battle of Hastings. He may have been wounded at the battle as he died shortly afterwards on 14 October 1066.

Matilda is thought to have been born around 30 November 1155 into a large family, which later included half-siblings from her father's second marriage to Eleanor of Domnart.

Men exercised near total control over women's lives during this period. A daughter like Matilda was essentially the property of her father, akin to a valuable asset which, upon marriage, could enhance his coffers or his position in society. Most aspects of her early life would be dictated by him: her upbringing, education, who she saw, where she went – all of which would influence her position in society. Upon marriage, her husband would effectively then assume a controlling position similar to that of her father before him.

Because of this status, women were often viewed as of little importance outside the domestic sphere and, as men overwhelmingly wrote the chronicles of the times, women did not normally figure in them. The only exceptions were women who became queens, or those who held a title or lands in their own right. Eleanor, Duchess of Aquitaine, was one such woman. She was unusual in managing to retain a degree of autonomy when she became queen upon marrying King Henry II.

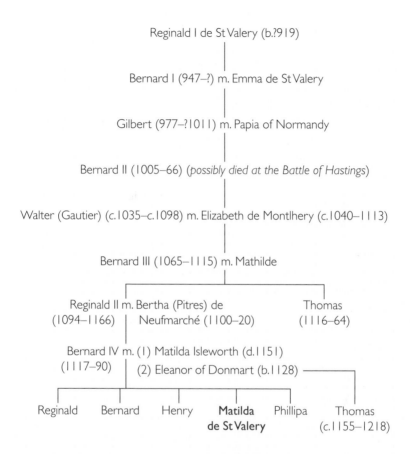

Reginald I de St Valery (b.?919)

Bernard I (947–?) m. Emma de St Valery

Gilbert (977–?1011) m. Papia of Normandy

Bernard II (1005–66) (*possibly died at the Battle of Hastings*)

Walter (Gautier) (*c.*1035–*c.*1098) m. Elizabeth de Montlhery (*c.*1040–1113)

Bernard III (1065–1115) m. Mathilde

Reginald II m. Bertha (Pitres) de          Thomas
(1094–1166)    Neufmarché (1100–20)      (1116–64)

Bernard IV m. (1) Matilda Isleworth (d.1151)
(1117–90)    (2) Eleanor of Donmart (b.1128)

Reginald    Bernard    Henry    **Matilda
                              de St Valery**    Phillipa    Thomas
                                                            (c.1155–1218)

Early records can be contradictory and dates unreliable, but this
family tree represents the most common interpretation of
Matilda's ancestry. It is now accepted that she was the daughter of
Bernard IV and not Reginald II de St Valery.[14] Her father married
twice. The number of her siblings is uncertain, but it is known that
Thomas was her half-brother from her father's second marriage.

A select de Valery family tree

Unlike Eleanor, Matilda held no titles or land, and as a consequence much about her early life remains a mystery. She was ignored by official documents which were primarily related to matters of finance and land-ownership.

Shortly after the Battle of Hastings in 1066, mention is made of the Saint-Valery family holding land at Isleworth in Middlesex, a small Saxon town on the Thames. Nearly 100 years later Matilda's father, Bernard IV, held extensive estates in this region, the principal one being at Hinton Waldrist in Berkshire (now Oxfordshire). It seems likely that, when she was a child, Matilda would have spent time at the family estate here. Matilda's mother (Bernard's first wife) had the surname Isleworth and it is possible that the original estate was her marriage portion.

Matilda's father would have expected his daughter to marry into baronial aristocracy. In such a position, she would be expected to manage not only her own domestic affairs but also her husband's estates while he was absent. Consequently, Matilda would have received some sort of education commensurate with these demands, including how to read and write. The generally accepted view, promulgated by the church, was that women were of limited mental capacity, and that too much education would overtax them.[15] Fortunately, this view was widely ignored, although sons generally received a broader education than daughters.

Matilda may also have been taught to play chess, which was seen as a social necessity (albeit with simpler rules than those played today).

Early learning for all children during this period was undertaken by the women of the household, and this included careful tutoring in good social etiquette. Later, it was usual for sons to be placed in the household of a 'man of experience' to learn skills including riding, combat, falconry and archery.

For daughters, their education would have continued at home, perhaps augmented by the local nuns or even a period at a convenient convent. Matilda may have gone to nearby Godstow nunnery, where her daughter Flandrina eventually became prioress.

## Matilda de Braose

Even once married, women during this period often remain absent from written sources. For most of Matilda's life, information about her was largely recorded only when she was involved in matters affecting her husband. As a consequence, details of Matilda's adult life are sparse, and because there were a number of women called Matilda de Braose (including her own daughter) confusions inevitably occur.

Matilda's own marriage was to William III de Braose, 4th lord of Bramber, and through this she became lady of Bramber. The date of the marriage is a matter of speculation. Matilda would have been able to marry from the age of 12 years, although the ceremony was often delayed until after puberty. This means the marriage probably took place around 1166–69, although later dates have been suggested.

Marriages at this level of society were often political affairs used to cement alliances, increase estates and acquire wealth. Neither the bride nor usually the groom typically had much influence in the matter. Although Matilda and William's compatibility has led to speculation that theirs was a love match, the primary reason for their alliance was probably political. It cemented the union of the powerful Saint-Valery family, who held estates in France, with the de Braose family, who by this time were largely based in England. The couple evidently formed a good team, and together they created one of the most important, and powerful, families in the realm.

Medieval life was generally not comfortable or straightforward for women. Under English law, women were subject to 'coverture', a situation that lasted unchanged for centuries.[16] With this, the woman ceased to be a separate being and everything she did was incorporated into and under the protection of her husband. A husband and wife became one person in law, although she was able to sue and be sued, and could legally appear as her husband's attorney.

Welsh women were in a different position. It is true that they were also subject to coverture, and unlike English women forbidden to own land under any circumstances. However, under the Laws of Hywel Dda they were treated more equitably in other ways than their English counterparts. Like English women they could not make contracts, but unlike them they could object to the terms of a contract and veto it if they felt it went against household finances. They also had rights of divorce if their husband became a leper, proved impotent or cheated on her three times. This was something denied English women. Even if they might live in Wales, and within the autonomy of the Marcher lordships, this freedom did not apply to Anglo-Norman women so did not affect Matilda.

Despite this handicap, woman like Matilda, with strong personalities, powerful friends, persistence and persuasion, could sometimes improve their positions. It was only on becoming a widow that a woman would become a citizen with increased rights.[17] She could be designated a guardian of her children, and was also entitled to a dower. This was the right of a widow to one third of her husband's land when he died. Given the number of relatively young women who married older husbands, this was an important right (though not one that Matilda was able to take advantage of, as she died about a year before her husband).

Matilda's marriage to William was a good one in that she gained much from it and had little to bring to it; although, as was normal procedure, her father bestowed a marriage portion on her. Matilda was given Tetbury in Gloucestershire. In effect, this was Matilda's share of her family inheritance.

By law, control of Matilda's marriage portion would have automatically passed to her husband, William. Tetbury was useful to William as it was in middle England where he did not originally have estates. While he was free to do what he liked with the estate, in the event of her widowhood Matilda would have regained control.

We know that William allowed Matilda to retain Tetbury for her own use, which was normal practice in influential families. Often a mother's marriage portion would be passed, in turn, to her daughter upon marriage.[18] Matilda was not able to pass Tetbury on to one of her daughters because, after the outlawing of William and Matilda, Tetbury was confiscated by King John, along with all the other de Braose estates.

## Married Life

Nothing is known about Matilda's early married life. There are no records of where she lived, of her domestic arrangements or how much she travelled. While travel was not without its dangers, voyages by sea to the Continent or Ireland were not uncommon among people of Matilda's status.

A baron like William, with extensive land holdings, would have been travelling a great deal of the time. He would have made extensive visits to his English estates and the land he held in France, as well as possibly occasional trips to Ireland. William also accompanied both Richard I and John to France on their expeditions to hold or enlarge the possessions of the English Crown.

While it seems possible that Matilda accompanied her husband to court on a number of occasions, there is no record of this. Was she with him on visits to his various estates? Again, we do not know. In particular, there is no record of her visiting Bramber in Sussex, the original seat of the de Braose lordship after the Conquest. William was constantly engaged in armed conflict, so it would not necessarily have been easy or safe for Matilda to accompany him all the time. Despite this, William must have returned to Matilda on a regular basis if the number of children they had is anything to go by.

At a time when families were often large, Matilda is credited with having had perhaps as many as 16 children, although some of them died in infancy. Proof of parentage is strongest for only ten of the children, but there is strong circumstantial evidence for the other six, and they are generally acknowledged to have been hers.

Matilda's ability to produce such a large family would prove a distinct advantage to her husband. The children of the couple married into influential families within the Marches, such as the de Lacys, the Mortimers and the de Clares. William was able to use these connections on occasion to witness grants or provide supervision of parts of his extensive estates. Despite subsequent events and the downfall of their parents, Matilda's children were ultimately able to escape punitive treatment, with some achieving powerful positions in their own right.

A noblewoman like Matilda would have controlled and administered her own household. William would have appointed bailiffs or stewards, known as seneschals, to run his estates. They would have been responsible for all the day-to-day running and administration, including the keeping of the accounts of both the household and estate. Matilda was a powerful woman in her own right and undoubtedly would have maintained an overview in William's absence.

In the process, if she thought that the seneschals were not doing their jobs properly, it is likely she would have intervened to ensure they did, or taken over herself. Reputedly, if there were disputes, she acted as arbitrator to ensure the protection of William's, and her, interests. Hay became her personal base and she oversaw the couple's interests there with great authority. As we shall see, Matilda even defended William's lands – militarily when necessary. Overall, William would have relied heavily on Matilda's administrative skills, and by all accounts she was more than capable.

As these were turbulent times, in order to ensure self-protection, William would have taken a personal entourage of knights and soldiers with him when on his travels. Similarly, Matilda would have had a guard of fighting men stationed with her as personal protection. This would have been particularly important in the volatile Marcher lands, such as those around Hay.

Travel would not have been easy for Matilda with such a large family to consider. Domestically, she is likely to have had nannies, who would have stayed with the family for succeeding births. Wet nurses were chosen from good families, so that they could pass on respectable values along with their milk to the infants. 'Rockers', the ladies employed to rock infants in their cots for hours each day, similarly stayed with families for extended periods. There would also be tutors for the older children, personal maids for herself, and myriad domestic servants such as housekeepers, cooks and housemaids.

With no such thing as ready-made clothes in this period, people had either to make their own or to arrange for them to be made. Having well-made and well-laundered clothes was a sign of status and would demonstrate to others that Matilda had staff to look after the family.

She would have had seamstresses to make her clothes from lengths of cloth, which she either bought herself or were acquired by William on his travels. Numerous garments would also have been needed for the children. Probably, one of the duties of her ladies-in-waiting would have been to assist the seamstresses.

As a sign of their status, lords and ladies would generally dress as finely as their money allowed. During Matilda's time the Sumptuary Laws had not been enacted. These restricted what types of clothing, as well as their colour and materials, different classes of the population could wear. The laws were designed to prevent extravagance, but Matilda would have been expected to have a fine wardrobe to reflect her position as lady to an important baron. Making clothes, repairing and adjusting them, and of course laundering, would have been a constant occupation in the household.

Typical garments for a wealthy lady in the late twelfth century were a linen shift that extended from collar to ankle. Over this she would have worn a kirtle – a tunic-like garment similar to a long shirt. The sleeves in particular were subject to the vagaries of fashion. At one time, as a sign of aristocracy, they were worn so tight that they had to be sown on, demonstrating that the owner had servants to assist with dressing. These were so impractical they later became looser and free-flowing. In this instance, aristocratic women wore them excessively long to denote their status. The kirtle was typically made of wool and was probably embroidered or decorated in some way. It would be drawn in at the waist with a belt.

Over the top of the kirtle, another long-sleeved tunic, or surcoat, would usually be worn, often lined with fur. Topping this off might be a mantle – a long cloak worn pinned high at the neck and again fur-lined. The weather in Wales can be wet and cold, and central heating was a luxury as yet undreamt of. As a consequence, warm, layered clothing, capes and cloaks were the order of the day, particularly when outside, travelling or hunting.

Whether or not women would have worn underclothes at this time remains a matter of debate. There are a number of references to, and illustrations of, men wearing underpants called 'braies' in medieval manuscripts. For a long time, it has been a commonly held belief that women had no under-garments in the modern sense until the nineteenth century. While this is generally accepted, in Lengberg Castle in Austria several garments resembling pants and bras have been discovered. These have been carbon-dated to the fifteenth century.[19] It is not known how widespread the use of garments such as these might have been in the twelfth century.

Ladies' headwear often comprised a wimple – a simple piece of cloth covering the hair, neck, cheeks and chin. Eyebrows were often plucked, and hair on the forehead partially plucked to make the forehead appear bigger. Hair was usually worn in two plaits, the longer the better, managed with ivory, bone or boxwood combs. Matilda would have had a small hand-mirror, possibly concave to give a full-face reflection. To achieve the pale 'English rose' look with rosy cheeks, rudimentary make-up, such as sheep fat mixed with a red pigment, was used, despite the disapproval of the Church.

Accounts from the time describe Matilda as a vigorous, formidable woman with a strong character, who was popular, although probably not with the Welsh. She was also considered beautiful and courageous, and known for her common sense and wise decisions.[20] Unfortunately, these qualities seem to have largely deserted her later when dealing with King John.[21]

## Matilda and William's Reputation

The only first-hand contemporary character reference we have for Matilda and William was written by Gerald Cambrensis, Gerald of Wales.[22] Gerald was probably born in c.1146 at Manorbier in southwest Wales. Fiercely ambitious, he was made archdeacon of Brecknock in 1176 at the age of 28, and based himself in the Archdeacon's Palace at Llanddew just outside Brecknock.[23]

Gerald's palace at Llanddew was within the lordship of Brecknock, which William was constantly fighting to hold against attack by the Welsh princes. Consequently, as archdeacon of the area, Gerald is likely to have met Matilda and William, and would have known about the local reputation of the couple.

Gerald had been made court chaplain to Henry II in 1184, and accompanied Prince John to France. Subsequently, he became critical of the Crown because of the court's bias against Wales and Welshmen. In 1176, on the death of his uncle, Gerald tried unsuccessfully to be appointed to the Bishopric of St David's. He was also unsuccessful when he tried again in 1198, despite travelling to France to remonstrate with Prince John just before he became king.[24]

At this time William was a court favourite and was present in France. While he would have been in a position to do so, we have no idea whether William tried to intercede to support Gerald's application. Gerald's claim was based on a legal technicality within the church administration but unfortunately he was opposed by the archbishop of Canterbury, Hubert Walter. Hubert seems to have convinced John that Gerald's application was fundamentally a political ploy to extricate the church in Wales from control by the church in England. John was never going to support this. Any attempts to plead Gerald's cause would have been in vain, even if William had wanted to help him.

Gerald is now best-known for his writings about his travels and the people he came into contact with. Unfortunately, we cannot always readily judge the accuracy of these texts as all we have are Gerald's accounts of these journeys and contacts. Current thinking is that he is an important chronicler of the age, providing valuable insights into everyday life and the lives of important people, though with some questions over the accuracy and impartiality of some of his writings. He wrote character sketches of the powerful people of the time, whom he came into contact with, and, while some of these sketches show an element of bias, overall they appear reasonably accurate.

It is thought that Gerald was probably able to understand Welsh, although he did not speak it and required an interpreter for complex speeches. Gerald travelled widely and wrote in Latin, as well as demonstrating an understanding of Greek, Hebrew, English, Irish, French and German. With all these language skills he would have been able to communicate with his Anglo-Normans overlords as well as the native Welsh. Although not uncritical of things Welsh, he was a devoted Welshman, as well as viewing himself as a man of the world.

Gerald described William as a good friend, although there are factors that may have influenced Gerald's attitude, such as William's good relationship with the Crown, and Gerald's ambitiousness. However, in the first version of his *Journey through Wales*, Gerald had been strongly critical of William, viewing him as an upstart. He wrote that William had been lucky to acquire his position, and that it had not been due to ability; William had been fortunate to benefit from the successes of others.

Later, he modified his writings, possibly due to fear of falling foul of such a powerful and ruthless baron. However, by the third manuscript version, rewritten after William's death, Gerald became critical again. This change of approach did not prevent Gerald recording that William admired him. Gerald felt this was for his daring defiance of the king, the archbishop of Canterbury and all the English clergy in his battle to be made bishop of St David's. Gerald also notes William's complimentary view about Gerald's family support for his impoverished nephew.

One incident reflects the conflicting information found in Gerald's writings. William had gained his fearsome reputation as the 'Ogre of Abergavenny' for an incident that occurred in 1175, when he was only around 20 years of age. William lured the local chieftain Seisyll ap Dyfnwal, his son Geoffrey and a number of Welsh princes with their wives and families, to a banquet in Abergavenny Castle on Christmas Day 1175. Ostensibly this was to settle collective disputes, including in relation to the death of William's uncle Henry de Hereford ten years earlier. Gerald states that the real reason for the event was for William to inform the Welsh that Henry II had decreed that no Welshman could bear arms in his domains. Regardless of the reason, all the Welshmen had been persuaded to leave their arms outside. At the banquet, William had all the 70 men and women massacred, and he then pursued and killed Seisyll's seven-year-old son Cadwaladr.

There is a view that the villain of this incident was William II[25] but it is more generally accepted that William III was responsible. It is possible that his actions were influenced by his uncle Philip de Braose and Ranulf Poer, the king's official in the Marches. Regardless of this, William III became known as the 'Ogre of Abergavenny'.

Gerald gives a full account of William's actions in his first writings. In the second and more supportive version he tells us William was not responsible. It was Ranulf Poer, the then sheriff of Hereford, who committed the massacre on the orders of Henry II.

This version of the events is not credited as trustworthy though it includes a reference to William being thrown into the castle moat. Gerald may have heard this from William himself as William later made the excuse that he had been tossed into the castle moat and only saved by his men. The origin of this story could have been an account of his narrow escape after the massacre, when the men of Gwent besieged the castle and killed the governor and his men. Matilda was not present at these events.

A modern author, Horatio Clare, has rewritten this story in the first person from the perspective of William.[26] Speaking in a forthright tone, Clare has William portraying this incident as a means of solving all his problems. He says Seisyll was a murderer who was always breaking treaties, and behaved towards everyone else with disdain and disrespect. He was a terrorist who needed eradicating so that the hills would become safe for law-abiding Anglo-Normans like William. Even if this was William's viewpoint it does not justify such a barbaric act.

In his writings, Gerald gives way to displays of vanity. He says of himself that as a young man he was naturally endowed with a handsome physique married with delicate features. We need to bear this in mind when considering the letters that he wrote to the Pope. In them, he says that Matilda had paid him a compliment on his good looks and had declared him the best of clerics in Wales, the equal of any man in erudite debate.

Whether this was a true reflection of Matilda's feelings or a slightly barbed comment we do not know. Certainly, Gerald took Matilda's views as a compliment, and they possibly influenced his observations about her. Initially, he reported that Matilda was thought to be arrogant by some. Later, he softened this opinion, and in an insight into her character he described her as prudent and as diligent in the economy of her housekeeping as she was enthusiastic in acquiring additional resources.

Gerald went on to wish Matilda temporal happiness and the glory of eternity. We know from his writings that Gerald was very fond of Llanthony Priory in the Black Mountains just south of Hay. Matilda is recorded as one of the founders who endowed its foundation, and this may have further influenced his judgement.

Other than Gerald's own accounts, nowhere is there any indication of Matilda's or her husband William's thoughts on the archdeacon. They may have tolerated rather than liked him, as Gerald vacillated between being antagonistic and then sycophantic towards them. His compliments may have been an attempt to gain their support for his future ambitions.

A more critical view of Matilda was given by a slightly later account of her in the *L'Histoire de Ducs de Normandie et des Rois d'Angleterre*. This important document records that her reputation was greater than that of her husband, and that it was Matilda who was the more aggressive in pursuing the Welsh and gaining new land from them.[27] Given William's reputation, this was quite a strong assertion.

William Camden, the noted antiquary, continued with this theme in his view of Matilda. In his book *Britannia*[28] he suggests that she was shrewd and impudently disrespectful, as well as making the personal comment that she was stout. (On what basis he formed this opinion we have no account, and the comment on her physique may well have been conjecture on her appearance in middle age after so much child-bearing.)

The other well-placed contemporary account of Matilda that we have is by Anonymous of Bethume, who confirms that Matilda was formidable. He also states that she was well-liked, as well as beautiful, valiant, vigorous and wise. He describes how she was always present at her husband's councils. Presumably, this would have been in Hay or the Wye Valley, as it's unlikely she could have travelled with him the whole time on his constant perambulations between his estates.[29]

In tracing Matilda's life, it has to be borne in mind that she was known by a number of names during her lifetime. The following are Anglo-Norman and Latin variations of her name. Matilda's Welsh names will be discussed in some detail later.

Matilda was named Maud at birth in France, but Matilda was a common anglicised version of the name in medieval times. Confusingly, either variation could occur concurrently, and in the case of 'our' Matilda there were also a number of suffixes used throughout the course of her life.

1.  MATILDA or MATHILDA DE SAINT-VALERY or VALERIE: her maiden name.
2.  MATILDA DE BRAOSE or BRIOUZE: her married name.
3.  MAUD DE HAYA or HAIA: seen in official documents in her later life.
4.  MATILDIS DE S. WALERICO/ WALERICUS: this was used in relation to endowments given to nearby Llanthony Abbey in the Black Mountains, and the gifting of St Mary's Church, Hay to the Priory of St John, Brecknock. The name is derived from *Sanctum Walericum*, the name of the monastery in the town of Saint-Valery, where Matilda was born.
5.  In later life, as witnessed by King John, Matilda was often simply referred to as the LADY OF HAYA/ HAIA/ LA HAIE/ HALE/ HAY.

Some of the variations of Matilda's name

The famous Buck engraving of Hay Castle of 1741

# CHAPTER 2

# Matilda – Hay Castle and the Welsh

B Y the time she reached middle age, Matilda had based herself at Hay Castle and the lands around it, just over the English border into Wales. It is widely believed that Hay provided Matilda with her principal source of income at this time. She must have accumulated considerable wealth, but about this we know little. We do know that she boasted to her nephew Baldwin of Bethune, who became Count of Aumale upon his marriage, that she had 12,000 cows. From them she said she had so many cheeses that if 100 men were besieged in a castle, they could use the cheese as ammunition and this would last for a month, if the men had the strength to throw them.

It may have been Matilda's idea to choose Hay, or William may have asked his wife to settle there to control the Wye Valley. In medieval times this was the southern gateway into Wales from England. It was safer than the northern route into Wales through Chester, which was overshadowed by the Welsh princes' domains in Snowdonia. Matilda would also have been well-placed to deter any incursion into England from the Welsh side. Matilda's presence in Hay ensured a secure base for William's recurrent excursions into mid- and south Wales as he continued the itinerant life of a Marcher lord.

Matilda appears to have been a confident and determined character. She is recorded as carrying on war against the Welsh in which 'she conquered a good deal'.[1] Reputedly, she was very tall and would wear armour in order to lead troops into battle – such as when she led her own army into Elfael (Radnorshire). This added to her reputation as it was considered scandalous at this time for women to wear men's clothes, even when out riding in inclement weather.

Painscastle: the massive stone fortress was built by Henry III in 1231 but demolished by Llywelyn ap Gruffudd in 1265 (© CPAT image 4236-3412, photo by Julian Ravest)

William took possession of the area round Painscastle in 1195 when the Marcher lords struck into central Wales. It is claimed that it was Matilda who led the forces that approached Painscastle in 1195, where she is credited with slaughtering the Welsh. The following year, however, it was eventually forced to surrender when besieged by the Lord Rhys of southern Wales. However, he came to an agreement with William de Braose – William assenting to withdraw from his attack on Ceredigion, and the Lord Rhys withdrawing from Painscastle.

The next attack, the famous siege of Painscastle, occurred on 22 July 1198, barely one year after Matilda's youngest child was born. This followed an incident during which William beheaded the Welsh Prince Talhaiarn, lord of Llangorse, after tying him to a horse's tail and dragging him through the streets of Brecknock. This angered the prince's uncle Gwenwynwyn, prince of Powys. He raised an army and in July advanced through Elfael and attacked Painscastle.

Matilda was in residence at the castle at the time and she led a spirited defence with her few retainers, holding out for three weeks. Fortunately for her, the Welsh were only armed with bows and arrows and had no siege engines.

The delay gave time for Geoffrey fitz Peter, the justiciar of England (and in effect the king's regent in his absence) to organise a Norman relieving force in Hay. On 13 August he attacked Gwenwynwyn and raised the siege, killing 3,000 Welsh attackers. The local tradition is that after the fight the River Bachawy ran red with blood, and a nearby Neolithic burial mound was referred to as their mass grave for a long time afterwards.

This incident appears to have added to the growing reputation of Matilda. Painscastle subsequently became known to the English as Castrum Mathilda, Maudcastle or Matilda's Castle – possibly partly as a result of her strengthening of the existing structure. Henry III later rebuilt the castle in stone. When he was in residence, from July to September 1231, the king signed his papers 'Maud Castle in Pain Castle'. While English chroniclers may have recorded that he repaired Maud Castle, Welsh records say that he repaired Castell Paen (Painscastle).

Another formidable woman who defended the castle but who did not achieve Matilda's fame was Petronella, Matilda's granddaughter. She was the daughter of Matilda's sixth child Margaret who married Walter de Lacy. Petronella was the wife of Ralph IV de Tosney, and was given the castle on her husband's death. Like Matilda, she stoutly defended it against a similar incursion by the Welsh in 1250. It shows the depth of feeling about Matilda that Petronella's action has been forgotten despite her acting in a similar way.

Matilda has always been strongly associated with building work at Hay Castle. Whether this was instigated as a result of concerns about the threat to her from the Welsh after the attack at Painscastle, we will never know.

## Hay Castle

There was a castle in Hay in 1188, as Gerald records that Bishop Baldwin stayed in a castle overnight on 7 March. This possibly could have been the motte and bailey structure near St Mary's Church, built by Sir Philip Walwyn a century earlier in 1088. There is no other recorded history of this site.

Years before the bishop's visit, Sir William Revell was given the lordship of Hay, and his name is linked to a castle. There is no primary evidence for this, and the location of this castle has never been conclusively established, but there are a number of theories.

He might have built a second motte and bailey castle, and if so, it was probably on the main castle site in the middle of town. Despite archaeology on the site, there are no conclusive indications of its precise location. One idea was that it could have been where the present coach house was built, but there are no clues to this on the ground.

An alternative possibility is that William may have been responsible for the square stone tower sited on the bluff above Castle Square. The square design is thought to be early and to date from around the 1120s to the 1140s, and almost certainly before 1200. The tower is now referred to as the keep and was the first stone building that we know of on the site.

If the keep tower was built at such an early date, it was just within the lifetime of Bernard de Neufmarché who died around 1125. Bernard had advanced along the Wye Valley and captured Brecknock where he built a castle. William fitz Osbern, the first earl of Hereford, had built a castle overlooking the Wye at Clifford a few miles from Hay, but that was in England. Bernard may have wanted his own castle over the Welsh border nearer Brecknock to secure his line of advance. Fortifications at Hay would do that. This may have been the 'castello de haia' received by Miles of Gloucester in 1121 when he married Bernard's daughter. Revell could have become the bailiff, or even completed the building of it, when he received the lordship.

The keep tower walls have been extensively rebuilt over the centuries, so it is difficult to be sure exactly what the structure originally looked like. There was certainly one, and probably two upper floors. As the biggest if not the only stone building on site at the time, it was the most defendable, and as a consequence the upper rooms would have been used for accommodation. Dendrochronology shows that the fireplaces you can see now date from the sixteenth century. This was when the keep tower was incorporated into a new house built adjacent to it on the site of the old castle Great Hall.

A period photograph of the keep from inside the castle walls (note how the level of the courtyard has been raised by around 6ft since the keep and gateway were built)

During the restoration work carried out in 2019, archaeologists found signs of two tufa stone arches internally at the base of the keep tower. These were blocked up many centuries ago but appear to have been original features. Their orientation on the north and south walls indicates that this was originally a gatehouse tower with large doors. Such a tower was a common feature of early medieval castles and it would have been the original way in. The castle bailey would have been built behind it on the bluff, and at this stage would probably only have been surrounded by a wooden palisade.

Today, this arrangement seems an unlikely way into the castle, given the steep climb up to the keep tower, but the slope was not always like this. The land contours were different before they were altered when the front terraces were landscaped in the early 1600s when the Jacobean mansion was built.

This keep tower at Hay Castle is smaller and simpler, but of a similar design, to gatehouses at Ludlow and St Albans. The original Ludlow Castle gatehouse was built in the eleventh century, with two doorways, one on either side at the base, and an arcaded passageway between them. This led into the castle. The upper chambers were used as living accommodation but were not accessible from the lower doorway. In the late twelfth century, changes to the layout were made. The outer gateway was blocked and the inner gateway rebuilt to a different configuration. The gateway was replaced by a new arched entrance and drawbridge built adjacent to it.

While the arrangements at Ludlow were more complex (as befitting a much larger castle) similar strengthening work was also done at Hay. A new gateway was built, adjacent to the tower, with a stone curtain wall around the site. This made the original gatehouse tower design obsolete. Blocking up the archways effectively made the gatehouse into the castle keep.

Normally, there was no access to the upper floors of tower gatehouses from the gateway passage. Access would be at first-floor level. The small door set halfway up the east keep wall at Hay, adjacent to the new gateway, may have been the original first-floor entrance, although the current design appears to be of a slightly later date. The sealed lower space could then become a dungeon or more probably a storehouse.

At Bury St Edmunds the abbey gatehouse was never modified. This shows how the original gatehouse towers at Ludlow and Hay might have looked, with arches either side at the base and big wooden doors which fold back internally against the sides of the tower.

While no evidence has yet been found of other buildings on the Hay site before 1200, we know that there would have been a bailey courtyard. This was a standard design feature of castles, and would have been used to hold store houses, stabling for horses, a smithy and kitchens. There must have been buildings here as in 1155 a charter by Earl Roger of Hereford granted a house within Hay Castle grounds to Brecknock Priory.

Notwithstanding what was originally on the site, the main stone castle gateway and the curtain walls we see today were later additions. Local legend has it that they were built around 1200, and Matilda has always been credited with their construction. The Marcher borderlands were constantly contested by the Welsh. If Matilda was to base herself in Hay, she would have felt safer behind substantial stone walls, particularly after her experience at Painscastle. We know that

Matilda became so closely associated with Hay Castle that she became known as the Lady of Hay. A letter from John dated 1212, refers to her as Matilda of Haya.[2]

A Victorian study of Frances Bevan, one of the daughters of Archdeacon Bevan who inhabited the castle mansion for over 50 years from the 1850s. The picture shows Matilda's imposing gateway and the individual gates, dating from 1340 (*left*) and 1640 (*right*)

## Matilda and the Welsh

William and Matilda were typical of many powerful Anglo-Normans, and seen by the Welsh as avaricious in their acquisition of additional land to increase their power, wealth and influence. According to Gerald, the Welsh valued land above all else. As a consequence, there was a constant background of conflict between the Normans and the Welsh as each tried to gain or retain land from the other.

King John might have bestowed estates on William – such as Skenfrith, White Castle and Grosmont – but William had to fight to acquire or to hold other lands. The indigenous Welsh princes contested this and we know that William was constantly fighting around Brecknock and Builth Wells. Not only was he acquiring land and reinforcing his baronial position, but he was also working to destroy any idea of Welsh independence.

It was expected that a lord such as William would always be ready to be involved in armed conflict, and that Matilda as his wife would support her husband. What is interesting is that a great deal of the hatred of the Welsh inhabitants was directed personally at Matilda. Gerald particularly mentions that Matilda, rather than her husband, was steadfast in her acquisition of additional wealth.

The wife of a Marcher lord would be expected to act as regent in his absence but Matilda went further and also took an active part in military affairs. Her involvement in the siege of Painscastle is well-documented. As a result of this action, she would have been held partly responsible for the resultant death of 3,000 Welshmen, and this would not have endeared her to the local population.[3]

Radnor Castle, constructed to dominate the local settlement and surrounding Radnor Plain (© CPAT image 4236-3409, photograph by Julian Ravest)

This enmity could have been increased because she was thought to be acting in an unladylike manner – including her actions in wearing men's apparel (possibly armour) and her direct involvement in fighting, such as her leading an army north of Hay into Elfael (Radnorshire). To this day, inhabitants of New Radnor (approximately 15 miles north of Hay) claim that it was Matilda who destroyed their castle. This is despite history showing it was destroyed around five times in only 80 years, and mainly by the Welsh.[4]

In this scenario, is it any surprise that the Annals of Margam record that Matilda and William were hated by the native Welsh population? In practice, however, it is highly unlikely that such underlying enmity would have troubled the couple in the slightest way.

Matilda's reputation might have been different if she had shown sympathy and understanding in her dealings with the local population, but we do not know how she treated them. Was she a considerate employer? Did she support and give alms to the poor and the weak? What was her attitude when passing judgement while acting as regent during William's absence?

While the Welsh population might have had good reason to despise Matilda, her reputation seems to have spread more widely. The statement in the *History of the Dukes of Normandy*[5] is telling – that she was responsible for keeping up the war with the Welsh. This may be more hearsay than fact, but equally it reflected Matilda's continuing reputation after a period of time, and even surviving the circumstances of her unfortunate death. This historical source is a French document so it might be expected to take a partisan viewpoint about a Norman family.

The new gateway and stone curtain walls that Matilda built at Hay Castle in around 1200 would have served two functions. They were without doubt an additional defensive measure. Also, being situated on this elevated position, these features would have dominated the area and so been a visual reinforcement of her power. Painting the walls white and displaying banners, or even pieces of captured armour, may well have stressed this.

The hatred for Matilda by the Welsh continued for centuries and is well-illustrated by a reference in *Burkes Peerage 1831*. A Welsh source is reported to have stated that all was well on the border until William married Matilda. She then had the opportunity to take revenge on the Welsh for the murder of her uncle Henry de Hereford, by instigating the massacre at Abergavenny.

This story has no credence. All other accounts, including that of King John, blame William for the event, but it does illustrate the level of grievance felt against her. In practice, the source possibly confused Matilda with Queen Matilda, the monarch who was the predecessor to John's father Henry II. Henry de Hereford was her supporter and he died in 1143 leaving no male heirs.

By all accounts, Matilda was very confident and assertive in her dealings with others. Partly as a consequence of her reputation, the Welsh characterised Matilda as a witch with supernatural powers. From this a number of legends arose about her, such as the building of Hay Castle in one night and the tossing of a stone across the Wye.

The Welsh referred to Matilda as 'Malt Walbee' in the Welsh-based stories and legends about her. A number of name variations were also used, such as 'Moll Wallbee', 'Moll Walbec', 'Mallt Walbri' and 'Maud Walby'. The origin of these names remains something of a puzzle. There was a figure in Brecknockshire folklore called 'Moll Walbec' who went around dropping stones and building castles. This could refer to Matilda, except that the 'Wal' part of her surname Walbec is said to derive from her father's surname, fitz Walter (Matilda's father's surname was Saint-Valery).

There is a record of a 'Mallt Walbi' who was described as 'a Brecknock virago and leader of a gang of freebooters' in Glamorganshire. Welsh translation does not seem to shed much light. Is this another misunderstanding?[6] The Welsh *pys walbi* is the name given to sweet peas, while the literal Welsh translation of 'wal' is wall, and a 'pec' is a dry measure. Neither seem to relate to Matilda in any way.

Another of these alternative names seems to sum up Matilda's reputation with the Welsh. One hundred years ago the Radnorshire name for Matilda was Malaen-y-Walfa meaning 'the fury of the enclosure'.[7] Allowing for Matilda's fierce reputation, there are two possible origins of the reference to an enclosure.

Firstly, Matilda's spirited defence of Painscastle when attacked by the Welsh army. It could be argued that the large compound in which the castle sat was a type of enclosure.

Secondly, the term 'enclosure' was derived from the place-name for Hay, Matilda's base. The name Hay has had a number of spellings over the centuries. They include 'Haia Anglicana' (English Hay), 'Haia Wallensis' (Welsh Hay), 'Haiam', 'Haya', 'La Haye', 'Sepes Inscissa' and 'Tentura Haie', but they all have a common connection.[8] To the Anglo-Saxons the area was 'Haeg', which means a clearing in land used for hunting, which would otherwise have been forested. Post-Conquest deer parks were given the generic term 'Haiae' which literally meant a game enclosure surrounded by a strong fence or hedge. An area known as Haywood lay to the west of the city of Hereford, and it appears to have extended as far as Hay. It was referred to as the ancient forest of de la Haye in Elizabethan times.[9]

Henry I used the name 'Castello de Haia Tallata' in a Royal charter dated April 1121, referring to the area near the church at Hay.[10] This later became 'La Haie Taillee' or the 'clipped hedge'.[11] The Welsh corrupted this to 'Y Gelli Gandryll', meaning a clearing of a hundred plots or a fragmented copse (in other words, open or divided-up ground within a wooded or fenced area).

Given her forays against the Welsh in Elfael, the name Malaen-y-Walfa seems apposite for Matilda, and places her within the context of her time. It therefore comes as no surprise that Matilda's reputation as a witch may have given rise to stories about her in local folklore, and hence the legends that followed. Her name might also have been used to frighten children. An example of this is an unsubstantiated story alleging that schoolchildren in Brecknock used to sing a rhyme 'Maude Walbee dirty hands'.

There is no evidence that the rhyme was current in the 1970s when it was recounted to Geoffrey Fairs,[12] but there is an earlier story from around 1860. At this time, mothers in Hay were said to scold their children for being 'dirty as Moll Walbee'[13] – a threat to the children perhaps, that Moll Walbee would get them if they did not wash their hands or keep them clean.

The imposing keep of Corfe Castle, King John's stronghold in Dorset and possible scene of Matilda's incarceration. Even the gunpowder of Oliver Cromwell's forces couldn't destroy its formidable walls in the seventeenth century (© P. Hume)

# CHAPTER 3

# Arthur of Brittany
# and the Wrath of King John

T HE death of Prince Arthur of Brittany was one of the most notorious episodes in King John's notorious reign.[1] It has also been
inextricably linked to the downfall of William and Matilda.

Henry II had four sons. The eldest, Prince Henry, predeceased his
father when aged 28 years (being crowned as heir and co-king, leading
to him being referred to as 'Henry, the Young King'). His next son
Prince Richard inherited the throne as Richard I, the Lionheart, but
he died at Chalus in 1199. Henry II's third son Prince Geoffrey should
then have inherited the throne, but he died before Richard. This left
only Henry II's youngest son, Prince John.

While John had a claim to the English throne, there also existed
another possible contender. Before he died, Prince Geoffrey had a son:
Prince Arthur of Brittany, Henry II's grandson. At this time the exact
laws of English succession were not established. There was uncertainty
as to whether nephew Arthur was the next in line, or whether it should
be brother John.

In 1199, Arthur was just 12 years old, he only spoke French and had
never left France. Despite this, on hearing of Richard's death, he immediately declared himself heir to the English throne. At the same time,
he claimed all the estates in France controlled by the English Crown. To
bolster his case, and obtain additional military and political support, he
did homage to the French Dauphin. The Dauphin supported Arthur's
claim and even betrothed his daughter Marie to him.

Back in England, Prince John felt he was the rightful heir. According to ancient custom in Normandy,[2] the younger son had precedent
over a nephew. However, the English barons had concerns about John.

He was viewed to be a sly, untrustworthy character, not helped by his previous treasonous actions against his brother Richard I. This made the barons uneasy.

Arthur did have his English supporters initially, but unfortunately for him the grand old veteran William Marshal of Striguil had a famous conversation with Hubert Walter at Vaudreuil on 10 April 1199. During this, William Marshal described Arthur as proud and haughty, and advised by traitors.[3]

John felt he was the heir and the choice of his father and brother, Henry II and Richard I. In this he had the support of William III de Braose. William lobbied hard to ensure that all the English barons were persuaded that it was better to have an Englishman rather than a French boy on the throne. The result of this inheritance dispute was that John and his barons had to do battle against the barons of Brittany, Anjou, Touraine and Maine. These latter barons supported Arthur's claim, and under the Dauphin they fought to deprive the Plantagenet empire of the English estates in France, which Arthur had commandeered.

In the early days of John's reign, William and Matilda were royal favourites. William accompanied John on campaign in France. William was with John when he went to raise the siege of Mirabeau in France on 29 July 1202.[4] Here, the 16-year-old Arthur, with the help of French barons Hugh and Geoffrey Lusignan, had taken the town and were at the walls of the castle, besieging Queen Eleanor of Aquitaine. She was Henry II's widow, John's mother, and Arthur's grandmother. By now she was old but still retained much of her influence, and would be a useful pawn in the power struggle.

Queen Eleanor had managed to get a message to John, telling of her plight. As a result, John made one of the most successful military actions of his life. In a lightning march with his army, he arrived outside the town of Mirabeau just in time, trapping the besiegers inside. William personally captured Arthur on 1 August 1202. At a stroke he had removed this threat to John's Crown. By capturing a number of French knights, he also greatly helped John's cause in France, as well as securing useful ransom money.

Despite the romantic pictures depicting him as a child, at 16 years of age Arthur was sufficiently mature to be conferred as a knight, an acknowledgement and symbol of his manhood. This had been carried out by the Dauphin, thereby usurping the role that was rightfully that of an English king. Captured knights, according to the code of chivalry of the time, were seen as valuable assets. They were allowed certain privileges in terms of accommodation and treatment before ransoms were paid and they were released.

Arthur, as heir-presumptive to the English throne, and being of aristocratic status, would have expected to be treated with this respect. While he would probably have had to endure a long imprisonment, eventually he would be released after a ransom had been paid. John did not extend this courtesy to him. When Arthur was younger, he had sworn allegiance to John. As a consequence, his actions in swearing fealty to the Dauphin and then fighting with him against John were treasonable, and John treated him accordingly.

Pope Innocent III summed up Arthur's actions by saying that, when he was captured at Mirabeau, he was no victim but a traitor to John, to whom he had sworn allegiance. Consequently, it would be in order for him to die the most awful of deaths without a trial.

John made himself Arthur's guardian, and put William in charge of him. Arthur was put into a deep dungeon at the Castle of Falaise, not far from William's French estates. John's chamberlain Hugh de Burgh was made Arthur's gaoler.

A few years later, Matthew Paris relates that John went to Falaise to reason with Arthur. He tried to get him to renounce his claim to the English throne, break his allegiance to Philip and join his English kin. It appears that Arthur arrogantly refused. Hugh de Burgh was a major source of information for Paris, so lending this story some credability.[5] In light of Arthur's unbending attitude, John sent men to Falaise to neutralise the threat to his Crown, by blinding and castrating Arthur. The intention was to ensure that he could never become a focus of support for rebels against the king.

Unhappy with this turn of events, Hugh de Burgh took action to protect his prisoner and to ensure that Arthur came to no harm. John's men were dismissed and Hugh suggested, unsuccessfully, that Arthur had died. We do not know if Hugh did this with William's knowledge and approval.

Whatever the intention, the result for John was bad. The news that Arthur might be dead led to a revolt in Brittany, which rapidly spread throughout John's remaining domains in France. Despite a subsequent denial, the damage was done and the rebellions effectively lost the English king his French empire with the exception of lower Aquitaine. This caused John, never a very happy man, to become even more morose and bad-tempered. William was aware of this. He escorted Arthur to John at Rouen and renounced his responsibility for supervising Arthur's captivity.

## The Death of Arthur

At Easter the following year, 1203, Arthur disappeared. The Annals of Margam Abbey and other contemporary accounts agree that John murdered Arthur in a drunken rage at Rouen on the Thursday before Easter, 3 April 1203. John then threw Arthur's body out of a window into the River Seine.[6] Arthur's body, weighted down by stone, may have sunk, but that did not stop it being discovered by a fisherman a few days later. He recognised the young knight and took him for a decent burial, probably by the nuns at Saint-Marie-le-Pres.[7]

In practice, Arthur's death may have been more premeditated than this account suggests. Geoffrey fitz Peter, the king's justiciar, and effectively his deputy when the king was out of the country, was summoned by John to France only twice. One of these occasions was at Easter 1203, when his visit coincided with the presence of other influential courtiers. Among them were William Marshal, Peter des Roches, William Brewer and Reginald of Cornhill.[8] This suggests an important decision had to be made.[9] There is no documentary evidence what this was, indicating that the subject was 'delicate'. It may have been a 'court' to decide Arthur's fate. Further circumstantial evidence suggests that Peter de Mauley, rather than John, could have perpetrated the murder.[10]

The Annals of Margam Abbey suggest William had a hand in the murder, although he was exonerated from direct involvement. However, it is open to debate whether the annals can be entirely trusted. They were written some years after the event, when the de Braose family were strong patrons of Margam. The family helped it to become the wealthiest of the Cistercian houses in Wales. As William was probably the source of the story, some of the Margam details may reflect this.

Regardless of whether he was directly involved, it is quite possible that he witnessed Arthur's death. It was perhaps coincidental that, around this time, John gave William land at Gower and Limerick, and a dispute at Totnes in Devon was resolved by John in William's favour. There is also conjecture that the gift of Skenfrith, Grosmont and White Castle was the result of pressure by William, or bribes for his silence, over the disappearance of Arthur. William certainly knew the details of the killing, and importantly John knew that he knew.[11]

The Annals of Margam Abbey largely cleared William of involvement, and John's bad reputation tends to support the Margam account of events. Their version is corroborated by similar accounts which appeared in the Chronicle of Coggeshall, the contemporary writing of Matthew Paris, and the writings of William the Breton.

John did not help his reputation when he imprisoned Arthur's sister Eleanor, the Fair Maid of Brittany, for the rest of her life.[12] Under the Salic laws of inheritance in France, even as a female she was Arthur's natural successor to his lands in England, Brittany, Anjou and Aquitaine. When John died, his successor Henry III also viewed his cousin a threat and so continued to imprison her. Eleanor was imprisoned from 1202 until her death in 1241, longer than any other member of the English royal family before or since.

## Downfall of William de Braose

However successful a baron was, the key to his power and position was the attitude and support of his king. Unfortunately, John was highly manipulative, capricious and vindictive. Numerous barons found to their cost they could not rely on the king's word, or their previous good record of service to the king.

As we have seen, in the early days of John's reign William was very supportive of him; indeed, his backing was a key factor in John gaining the throne. In return, John favoured William by making him a key adviser and granting him extensive estates. This relationship lasted from 1198 until around 1208 when, for some reason, William fell foul of his monarch.

The downfall of the de Braose family was a key event in John's reign and the reasons for it have been the subject of extensive speculation ever since. Matilda has always had the blame laid firmly at her door because of a well-documented incident that occurred at her castle in Hay.

By 1207 John's support for William was becoming lukewarm. In 1208 he started to press William for some of the great deal of money William owed the king. An example was William's debt for John's grant of the honour of Limerick to him in 1201. In return for the grant, William agreed to pay the king 5,000 marks at a rate of 1,000 marks per year. However, by 1207 William had paid just 700 marks.[13]

John started to lose his patience and, in such circumstances, his usual practice was to 'invite' the heir to the lordship, and possibly any male grandchildren, to court. They effectively became hostages to ensure loyalty and compliance. Even loyal supporters were not immune. John demanded the eldest son of William Marshal as a hostage when relations between them broke down after Marshal was sent to parley with King Philip of France after Philip had launched a sustained, successful attack on the English possessions in his country in 1203. First Anjou was taken and then Philip advanced on Normandy. City after city fell. John was keen to sue for peace to stop Philip's advance and sent William Marshal to the French court to negotiate with the king.

Philip, however, was on a winning streak and refused to come to any agreement. Instead, he issued an ultimatum to the English barons with lands in France. Either they paid homage to Philip or their lands would be confiscated. Marshal, mindful of his extensive French holdings, paid homage to Philip.

When he returned to report to John, Marshal received a stormy reception. Not only had he failed to find a compromise with Philip, but found himself accused of treachery by paying homage.

John had no option but to organise a relieving force to send to France in order to protect his possessions. Marshal refused to join the expedition to Poitou, thereby hoping to retain his estates by not going to fight Philip. This made John unsure of Marshal's loyalty so he looked for reassurance by requesting Marshal's son come to court, in effect as a hostage. Marshal's wife Isabella warned him against agreeing to do so, but he had no choice.

Two years later, in 1206, Marshal planned an expedition to Ireland to strengthen his hold on his lands at Leinster. After initially agreeing, John subsequently refused Marshal permission to go. To persuade Marshal not to defy his wishes, John requested another hostage, his 12-year-old second son Richard. This time Marshal heeded his wife's warning and was able to circumvent the royal summons for a time.[14]

Records show that he was able to delay this sending of his son for a further 12 months. This account was either an error on the scribes' part or it shows Marshal defied the king for a time.[15] If so, this was a diplomatic triumph of sorts, as a refusal after his public quarrel with his king would have amounted to declaring himself a traitor and resulted in the confiscation of his lands.[16]

Taking hostages in this way was a royal tactic for centuries, done to ensure loyalty from powerful barons, and a favourite ploy of John. He also had an ignominious reputation where this was concerned. An extreme example of his treatment of hostages taken from those who disobeyed him occurred in 1212. John was planning a campaign in France when Llywelyn ab Iorwerth rebelled again. John had to divert his large French invasion force to Chester to counter this. John already held 28 sons of Welsh chieftains as hostages after a previous rebellion. In his rage he had all the hostages hanged when their fathers joined Llywelyn's rebellion. One was a child just seven years old.

By employing a mixture of astute judgement, luck and skill, Marshal managed to survive the reign of King John. In William's case, however, things did not go so well. William had pledged his grandson as a hostage for the debts he owed.[17] John followed this up by sending his messengers to Hay where Matilda was in residence. They requested that William and Matilda's eldest son and heir William IV, as well as their grandson William V, accompany them back to court. What happened next was pivotal in William and Matilda's future relationship with John.

According to the contemporaneous account by Roger of Wendover, Matilda provocatively refused. Matilda's words are widely quoted although her exact wording must be a matter of conjecture. According to Wendover, 'with the sauciness of a woman', Matilda refused the royal messengers, citing that the king had 'basely murdered his nephew … Whom he ought to have kept in honourable custody'.[18] Whatever Matilda's actual words, this incident appears to carry some truth and was widely reported, including in the Annals of Margam.[19]

William immediately tried to cover up his wife's impetuous remarks. He rebuked her and told her that she had spoken 'incautiously against her lord and king', but despite William's attempts to make peace overtures this proved a gross diplomatic error. John's furious reaction was to launch a sustained vendetta against Matilda and William. The couple were outlawed and William's estates were confiscated.

While Matilda's imprudent remarks have always been cited for John's extreme reaction, there are a number of alternative possibilities. These have been the subject of vigorous debate ever since.

## 1. Breaking an oath of secrecy?

As discussed above, the taking of hostages to ensure loyalty was an established and legitimate ploy by royalty. In this case, the only surprise to other barons was that John demanded it of his close supporter William de Braose. They would also have been aware of the rumours about Arthur's disappearance, although no one was likely to mention the subject in the king's presence.

Unfortunately, the way Matilda spoke with conviction about John's involvement in Arthur's murder suggests that William had confided some details to her. John may have felt William had broken an oath of secrecy, and who else might he have told? Regardless of that, once the story of Matilda's response started to circulate it would confirm any previous speculation about this among the barons.

Was this enough to result in William and Matilda being outlawed? Possibly not in itself, although John could be vindictive. What seems beyond doubt is that, when coupled with other factors, it would have been a strong contributory factor.

## 2. Owing a large debt to John?

John was always avaricious, but after he lost his domains in France when he first came to the throne, his desire for money increased further. Ostensibly, he was anxious to raise money to regain his lost estates, and he worked hard to maximise his revenue-raising capabilities. This took many forms. He charged widows if they wanted to stay single, and he charged them if they wanted to remarry someone of their own choice and not as directed by the king. He increased scutage, the fee paid by knights to avoid military service, and the fee for inheriting their family estates.

When the king, in his largesse, gave lands or properties to his barons, they were still expected to pay a fee to the king for them. John may have given the castles of Grosmont, Skenfrith and White Castle to William, but he was still required to pay 100 marks in money, three war horses, five hunting horses, 24 best bucks and ten greyhounds for them.[20]

William was no different to a number of other barons in owing the king vast sums of money. Also like a number of the barons, William was a slow payer, despite being one of the most wealthy and influential barons in the country. In 1206 he offered the king 10 bulls and a number of cows as a fee to avoid a task John had set him. William never attempted to pay this debt.[21] It may be that William felt that he had no obligation to pay as he had been a strong supporter of John over the years. Regardless of this, it was the expected practice that kings would not pursue their barons for these huge debts.

John was different. He was not above asking for payment. In 1207 he confiscated the lands of the earl of Leicester over non-payment of a debt.[22] In 1208, meanwhile, despite years of loyal service, it was William's turn. In 1212 John wrote a long letter in the Black Book of the Exchequer, justifying the action he took against Matilda and William. He said that he acted by 'the law of the exchequer' and claimed it was 'according to the laws and custom of England'.[23] The letter claimed that William was tardy in paying a fine of 50,000 marks, of which 5,000 marks were for lands given to him in Limerick. Altogether, this was a colossal sum which must have been built up over a considerable number of years.

Whatever his justification, such a letter of explanation by a monarch can only be viewed as a sign of the king's anxiety about the actions he took against them both. Possibly he had later misgivings about how his treatment of William was viewed by other barons. It is interesting that, after John had appropriated all the de Braose estates, he failed to collect from them all the money he claimed William owed.

### 3. John's insecurity about William's loyalty?

For any monarch the loyalty of a core number of barons was key to the monarch's ability to reign. These core supporters could also be used to counter any barons whom the king distrusted. In the early part of his reign, John was in dispute with Ranulf, earl of Chester and stepfather to Prince Arthur of Brittany. Giving support to William acted as a check to Ranulf and helped ensure that the Marcher lands were kept secure.

By 1204, John had lost his French domains. Before he could return to regain them, he had to be sure his kingdom was secure. The dispute with Ranulf was resolved the following year and he no longer posed a threat. This meant that there were no strong individuals to counter the power that William was building up in the Marches. Worryingly for John, by 1207 William was showing sympathy with other barons, notably his friend William Marshal, in their disputes with the king.

John may have begun to worry that the independence of the powerful Marcher lords, and in particular William, was a threat. By removing William, John was able to appoint mercenary knights to control William's estates and so reduce any threat of rebellion.

### 4. Events in Ireland?

For some historians it was events in Ireland that were at the root of the problem.[24] Like most Norman barons, William spent much of his time travelling around his estates. However, to look after his Irish holdings William was able to come to an agreement with Hugh de Lacy, the father of his son-in-law, Walter de Lacy. Hugh had fallen out with John early in his reign and retired to Ireland. There he agreed to look after the de Braose estates, while William performed a similar service for Hugh in the Marcher lands.[25]

In 1207, as part of plans to increase his revenues, John started to reorganise the administration of Ireland along English shire lines.[26] This included William's estate at Meath. The reorganisation meant that Meath would be removed from William. As a consequence, William vigorously resisted the energetic attempts of John's representative, justiciar Meiler fitz Henry, in this respect.[27] Meiler was undertaking his task with enthusiasm[28] as he shared the views of his cousin, Gerald of Wales, that William was an upstart.

Events in Ireland started to spiral out of control. A general uprising of the barons against Meiler ensued, and William complained to John about his treatment. This forced John to summon the barons to court and come to terms with them. Ever the diplomat, William Marshal attended but William refused to go to court and retired to his Welsh lands. It took an army under the sheriffs of Gloucester and Shropshire to force William to come to terms with the king.

## 5. Alliance with the Welsh princes?

John later said that he declared William an outlaw for forming an alliance with Llywelyn ab Iorwerth, king of Gwynedd, and ultimately ruler of the whole of Wales. While it is true that William formed such an alliance, this was in 1210 and only after his outlawing.

With some minor Welsh princes, William staged a mini-revolt on the Welsh-Herefordshire border. It achieved little. Leominster was taken and burned but they were unsuccessful in regaining William's castles in Hay, Brecknock and Radnor. There had been a number of earlier alliances with Welsh princes but these were all characteristic of life on the borders. They were a normal part of the Marcher lords' creative attempts to hold their lands, or increase their control of the region, or just to try and keep the peace.

## 6. *Burke's Peerage*

*Burke's Peerage 1831* states that a monk from Llanthony Priory believed that John acted as a result of William's persecution of the Welsh prince Gwenwynwyn. There is no veracity in this suggestion. John had summoned Gwenwynwyn to court at Shrewsbury in 1208, deposed him and seized his lands. This had nothing to do with William, and occurred before John's attack on the de Braose estates.

## The de Braose downfall

Whatever the real reason for John's displeasure, Matilda must have realised her error. She tried to placate John by sending a present to his second wife, Isabella of Angoulême. Her very expensive gesture consisted of 400 pure white White Park cattle and a bull with red ears. John was not appeased. (Similar White Park cattle can still be seen at Dinefwr Park where Matilda's daughter, also named Matilda, married one of the princes of Deheubarth.)

This was a difficult time for John. He was in dispute with the Pope, and his barons were showing signs of unrest. Matilda's outburst was general knowledge among the barons so it was essential to show strong leadership and act decisively in the face of such insubordination.

John acted swiftly, outlawing William and Matilda in 1208, confiscating their lands and seizing Hay, Brecknock and Builth Castles. For this, John employed foreign mercenaries, headed by Girard d'Athée, whom he made sheriff of Hereford and Gloucester. He even sent the bill for their services, amounting to 1,000 marks, to William. Girard was succeeded as sheriff by Engelhard de Cigogné, who later became Matilda's goaler.

William, Matilda and their son William IV (widely known as William Gam or Squinting Will), with other family members, were forced to flee into Wales. They travelled through the Gower to Pembroke and then escaped to Ireland.

A number of Marcher lords had established estates in Ireland from the time of Henry II's invasion in 1171. Henry made himself king of Ireland and established a strong royal foothold in the south and east, his crown estates including Dublin, Waterford and Wexford. Loyal, energetic Norman barons who had accompanied him, like fitz Gilbert and de Lacy, were granted lands. Richard Strongbow, a member of the de Clare dynasty, took Leinster, and this later passed to William Marshal. Hugh de Lacy held Meath and later William de Braose was given Limerick by John.

Over time, there was a good deal of intermarrying with Irish princesses by the early settlers as they gradually gained control of new lands and pushed the native Irish to the fringes of the country. The Irish were generally disparate and disunited, fighting against the self-contained and well-organised Norman barons. All this bred a degree of sturdy independence and autonomy in the barons, free from the confines of the allegiances necessary on the mainland. With no strong or unified leadership from either the Irish or Normans, Ireland did not pose a significant threat to royal power.

This royal indifference to Ireland meant that the estates there provided a useful refuge for those barons who had fallen out with John. In turn he found it expedient to let them live in relative peace as long as they paid their royal dues on time to his representative.

William's Limerick estate had been confiscated for John by Meiler fitz Henry, so William, Matilda and their family were offered protection by William Marshal, earl of Pembroke, on his Irish estate. After three weeks John Gray, who had replaced Meiler, complained to John that Marshal was harbouring a traitor. Marshal replied that he was just complying with feudal law requiring him to shelter his lord. This claim was vaguely plausible only if Marshal held any land in Wales under William's lordship.

Nevertheless, aware of John's ruthlessness, Marshal felt discretion was the better part of valour, so moved William and his family on to Trim Castle. This was held by Hugh II de Lacy, the younger brother of Walter de Lacy of Weobley and Ludlow, a family into which their daughter Margaret de Braose had married. With his family safe, William then returned to Wales on John's promise of safe conduct. William and John had a meeting at which John placed all the blame for their troubles on Matilda, and suggested they both return to Ireland and sort their problems out.[29] William refused and escaped to hide in Wales. John, now at almost the height of his power, decided to pursue Matilda and remove any de Braose sanctuary in Ireland.

John had been to Ireland before. His father Henry II had named Prince John as king of Ireland in 1177, and in 1185 John visited the country. While his visit was not a great success, he did manage to reorganise some administration along English lines, and granted further Irish land to his Norman knights. Ireland subsequently became an important source of exchequer funds for John throughout his reign.[30]

In 1209, in order to secure his back, John ensured that William would receive no help from William the Lion in Scotland. At the head of a big army, John headed north and negotiated the Treaty of Norham. By this, William the Lion agreed to pass over his two daughters for marriage into the English royal house, and paid £10,000. John was then able to set his sights on Ireland and invaded in 1210.[31]

Elaborate preparations had been made and the invasion army consisted of 800 knights and an army of Flemish mercenaries carried in a 700-ship flotilla. Such a formidable force was unnecessary on military grounds, given the disparate nature of the Irish resistance. John's expedition seems to have had two objectives. One was to put his troublesome English barons in their place and bolster his relations with the Gaelic chieftains. The other, it is assumed, was as a rehearsal for his plans to campaign in France to recover his lost lands.

John sailed from Pembroke and landed at Crook near Waterford in June 1210. He then moved through Newbridge and Thomastown to Marshal's castle at Kilkenny. All those in Ireland, Norman and Irish, saw that resistance against such a force was futile. Marshal made peace with the king, and fed his army for some time and at considerable expense.

Meanwhile, Walter also soon realised that opposition to the king was in vain, and so William, Matilda and family were again passed on, this time to Walter's brother Hugh de Lacy, earl of Ulster. After his stay with Marshal, John pressed on and by 28 June he was in Dublin. Here he dispossessed Walter of his estate in Meath, for harbouring William. Hugh made a half-hearted attempt to defy the king, but it was in vain and John chased him into the mountains of Mourne.

Showing strong leadership and confidence, John sent his army across Carlingford Lough on a bridge of boats and took the castle of Dunrum. In the face of such aggression, resistance was pointless. Hugh was forced to flee with the de Braoses to his fortress at Carrickfergus.

Again, William tried to come to some agreement with the king but John was not interested. In frustration, William returned to Wales.

There, he staged a small, ineffectual rebellion by forming an alliance with the Welsh princes. Apart from burning Leominster, it achieved little and the rebellion rapidly fizzled out.

Meanwhile, Matilda was desperate. Deserted by William, she tried to escape with her son William IV, accompanied by his wife and children. Also in the party were her son Reginald and daughter Annora, together with Hugh de Lacy. They all escaped by ship to the Isle of Man.[32] After four days Matilda and her entourage then moved on to Galloway in Scotland.

There are vague references in Irish and Manx sources that suggest John or his forces pursued them to the island. When he found they had fled, there is a suggestion that he took some sort of revenge on the islanders, though actual details are scarce. In Galloway, Matilda, Annora and William IV's luck ran out. They were captured by Duncan of Carrick. He returned them in chains, or possibly in cages[33] according to some reports, to Carrickfergus and to King John. For this Rhymer's *Foedera* records that Duncan was rewarded with a grant of Larne and Glenarm, and 50 carucates of land.[34] Matilda's son Reginald and Hugh de Lacy succeeded in escaping into Scotland and eventually they made their way to France and to safety.

John stayed on in Dublin, enjoying his victorious campaign and taking his customary hostages to secure future peace in the area. Once again Matilda tried to negotiate with him. John offered to release them, and pardon William, for a ransom of 50,000 marks. This was a totally unreasonable sum, more than the total yearly income of the English exchequer. Matilda insisted on seeing her husband and William was allowed to return under safe conduct to speak to her. Despite this the money was never paid. They were either unwilling, or more probably unable, to pay.

William eventually escaped across to France disguised as a beggar. He made his way to Paris where his son Giles, bishop of Hereford, and other clergy lectured at the college established there by exiled Englishmen. William died a pauper at Corbeil, Marne, Champagne-Ardenne shortly afterwards on 4 September 1211. He was buried in the Abbey of St Victoire, Paris, Isle-de-France.

William's funeral service was taken by Stephen Langton, archbishop of Canterbury, who had been forced into exile through John's disagreement with the Pope. John had not accepted the Pope's nomination of Stephen as archbishop of Canterbury. As a result, the Pope placed an interdict on England in 1208, banning clergy from taking any church services, and preventing them from performing baptisms or burials. When John insisted that the clergy ignore the interdict, senior clerics fled the country. The archbishop's involvement in William's funeral again incensed the king.

Meanwhile, on 26 August John returned from Ireland, through Fishguard. Matilda and her family were imprisoned at Bristol, and then she and her eldest son and heir William IV were moved to Windsor. An early report alleged they were starved to death by the castellan,[35] a foreign mercenary called Engelhard de Cigogné.

This report may have arisen slightly later, being taken as an opportunity to blacken Engelhard's name due to the enmity caused by John's use of foreign mercenaries (rather than strictly relating to Matilda).

Girard d'Athée was a French mercenary captain of low birth, who rose to almost baronial status in England. Not only was he employed by John for most of his reign, but he also brought many relatives and friends to England with him. Although they received few titles or estates, they worked together and supported each other to the envy of the English barons. They remained fiercely loyal to John, helping him to carry out the outlawing of the de Braose family. As a consequence of this unwavering loyalty, they were greatly despised.

One of them was Engelhard who assumed significant power under John's patronage. When Girard died in 1210, Engelhard succeeded him as sheriff in Hereford and Gloucester. This was de Braose country and Giles in particular hated him.[36] The barons wanted a number of these mercenaries dismissed from the realm, and Engelhard was one of those specifically named in Clause 50 of the Magna Carta of 1215. In this they were not immediately successful as he did not leave until 1224.

It is now generally believed that from Windsor, Matilda and her son were taken on to bleak, lonely Corfe Castle in Dorset. This was in John's favourite hunting ground of Purbeck and was very secure.

Only one access road from Wareham led to the castle. Ironically, Wareham had been one of the estates awarded to William IV's great, great-grandfather William I de Braose by William the Conqueror after the Norman Conquest.

This imposing castle was a place that John used on more than one occasion to keep hostages. After the death of Arthur, he imprisoned Princess Eleanor, 'Maid of Brittany', here (among a number of other places) together with 25 of her loyal French knights. They made an unsuccessful attempt to escape and as a result 22 of them starved to death, preferring that fate to more time spent in this forbidding fortress.

Somewhere within the castle, John disposed of Matilda and her son by immuration, leading to death by starvation and dehydration. The exact methods used to do this have varied throughout history. Often the victim was placed in an oubliette (from the French for 'to forget'), a sometimes bottle-shaped dungeon, the only entrance to which was through a hole in the ceiling. This would be far out of reach, so effectively there was no exit from the cell.

Traditionally, it has been claimed that Matilda and William were walled up. Technically this meant being encased inside a stone wall, and would have meant permanent oblivion. In their case a dungeon was said to have been opened after 11 days, so this would indicate that they were put into a cell, the door was locked and they were then left to their fate. Reports say that a sheaf of wheat or oats and a side of raw bacon were put in with them. The reason for the side of bacon is unclear and may have no intended meaning. The sheaf of wheat may have had a religious significance.

Reputedly, the chamber was opened after 11 days, on 9 August 1210. This would mean that they were incarcerated on 29 July. This was just two days before Lughnasad, the Celtic festival of regrets and farewells, but celebrated as Lammas in the Christian church. Traditionally, this marks the beginning of harvest when a sheaf of wheat was cut, milled and then baked into a loaf of bread.[37]

The first day in August was also the festival of St Peter in Chains, when St Peter was miraculously delivered from prison. This was a feast day about which John and Matilda would undoubtedly have known.

More prosaically, three sheaves of wheat were the symbol on the de Braose coat of arms. Was the inclusion of the wheat a reminder of this by John, and additional mental cruelty intended for Matilda?

Whatever John's motive was, the outcome was inevitable. When the chamber was opened, both Matilda and her son were dead. William IV was seated facing the wall with his mother's arms around him kissing his cheek. There is conflicting belief about whether closer inspection revealed that her son's cheeks were half-eaten.[38]

An alternative story, by Anonymous of Bethune, claims that it was Matilda's cheeks that had been nibbled by her son. Whatever the truth, this was the tragic fate of one of the most spirited, powerful and outspoken Norman ladies in medieval England: cruelly starved to death with her son, while her husband fled to die a pauper in a foreign country.

Other members of the de Braose family fared better. After a period of captivity or exile, they were all released or returned to England and resumed their normal lives. Her eldest sons, Reginald and Giles, petitioned relentlessly for the restitution of the de Braose family estates. John agreed to give back some but in practice he was tardy in doing so. Nevertheless, gradually much was returned, and John's successor Henry III looked favourably on the family when he came to power.

It is interesting that there was little overt opposition to the king's actions. This was despite William's extensive estates, political connections and his daughters' marriages into some of the most powerful baronial families. The minor acts of support by barons, such as Hugh de Lacy at Trim, were forgiven by John soon afterwards.

## Repercussions of John's actions

John has become renowned for his cruelty, his treachery and avarice. While some of this may be exaggeration, much appears to be true. John's reputation for vindictiveness arose during his lifetime. His destruction of Matilda and William, the leading baron in the Welsh Marches, and his confiscation of the de Braose estates, was an example of this and has been described as the greatest mistake of his reign.

His action against William, and particularly in the tragic end of Matilda, lady of Bramber, created additional problems for him. The removal of William created a power vacuum. John took control of the Marches by putting foreign mercenaries in place but he could not be present the whole time. This enabled the Welsh princes to take advantage, such as when Llywelyn ab Iorwerth rebelled in 1212.

It was not only the demise of William but also the severity of his downfall that heightened the mistrust of John felt by the barons. This dogged the later years of his reign,[39] and was compounded by the barons' concerns about John's treatment of Arthur.

It was not until 1216 that John was generally acknowledged to have killed Arthur, but all the earlier uncertainty had led to many embellished stories of what may have happened. This contributed to the general mistrust of the monarch, and ultimately to many major barons deserting him. All these were factors leading up to the first Magna Carta of 1215.

## Battle of Bouvines

The Battle of Bouvines on 27 July 1214 was devastating for John. It was the concluding battle of the Anglo-French war of 1213–14 between King Philip Augustus of France and John's nephew the Holy Roman Emperor Otto iv. Considerably aided by the lavish financial support of his uncle, Otto's army consisted of a confederation of European nobles, which included John himself. Unfortunately, at the key moment John's southern allies and the Poitevin barons proved untrustworthy. They fled. For three hours the battle raged first one way and then the other, but eventually the French won. The result profoundly influenced the course of history in France, England and the Holy Roman Empire.

For John the battle was disastrous. After extorting massive sums of money from his subjects, he lost it all, and with it almost all of his remaining possessions in France. This was another pressure contributing to the signing of the Magna Carta, and ultimately it led to the end of the Angevin Empire.

In a way, this battle was poetic justice for Matilda, even though she was dead by this time. Her half-brother Thomas de St Valery was in the victorious French army. He may have viewed the result of the battle as just retribution for the tragic manner of his sister's death.

An early twentieth-century photograph showing the keep with the original Boyle mansion (built around 1570) buttressed against it. The keep was incorporated as part of this early house before the house was rebuilt and expanded 70 years later, into the Jacobean mansion we see today

# CHAPTER 4

# Matilda's Family
# and Religious Influences

T HE de Braose family has been studied extensively but despite this
the number of children who can be securely attributed to Matilda
and William remains unclear. Records are sometimes incomplete, with
dates of birth not recorded or lost. In the absence of secure records,
inference is often needed in order to arrive at approximate dates of
birth (thus, the assumption that William, the oldest son, was born not
long after the couple were married). Dates of death are shown more
consistently, though many children at this time died young, with mor-
tality rates of 25–40% being common. Most authorities agree that the
couple had at least nine children (four sons and five daughters); while
others put the number as high as sixteen.

Part of this confusion is due to the recurring use of the same names
– particularly Maud/ Matilda and William – for different members of
the family and over a number of generations. In addition, the same individuals are often referred to by different names in different languages,
including Norman, Latin, English or Welsh. Many had variations of
their name in use at the same time, and within the context in which
they were used, the name could refer to other individuals or generations.

The following list is partly based on the de Braose genealogy given
in the thirteenth-century manuscripts on the history of the lords
of Brecknock collected by John of Wallingford.[1] As well as showing
Matilda's children, the genealogy demonstrates how important marriages could be in medieval times. By marrying their offspring to other
prominent families, barons were able to enhance their power base and
social connections. The de Braose children, both male and female,
married into some of the most important families in the Marches,

both English and Welsh. Equally important, politically speaking, were those members who chose a religious life. They included a bishop, an abbess and two highly regarded anchoresses.

The children for whom parentage is fairly certain:

Maud (Matilda) (c.1172–c.1210)
m.1189 Gruffydd ap Rhys II (d.1201), prince of Deheubarth, the son of 'The Lord Rhys'.

Gruffydd tried unsuccessfully to mediate in Matilda's battle at Painscastle between Gwenwynwyn and Geoffrey fitz Peter.[2] Maud was Gruffydd's second wife. They had two sons: Rhys and Owain, and a daughter Leuca.

William IV de Braose (c.1175–1210)
(Also known as Gwilym Gam or Squinting Will).
m. Maud (Matilda) de Clare, daughter of Richard de Clare, 3rd earl of Hertford and Amice fitz Robert de Meullant.

William and Maud had four sons, all of whom were eventually placed in captivity, not being released until 1218. Although they should have inherited, they did not. Whilst they were in captivity, the de Braose lands were reclaimed first by their uncle, Giles, bishop of Hereford, the second son of William III, and after Giles' death in 1215, by the third son, Reginald. Although William IV's four sons were released in 1218, Reginald's grip on the de Braose lands was secure. One of the brothers, John, attempted a legal claim to the family inheritance. Although this failed, he did succeed in acquiring the lordship of Gower and subsequently purchased Bramber from his uncle Reginald. William starved to death with his mother Matilda.

Loretta (Lauretta) (c.1176–c.1266)
m. Robert (fitz Parnell) de Breteuil (de Beaumont), 4th earl of Leicester.

Loretta's nephew Simon de Montfort, 5th earl of Leicester, was the father of the Simon de Montfort who led the insurrection against Henry III.

## Margaret (c.1177–c.1255)[3]
m. Walter de Lacy, 6th baron Lacy of Trim Castle and sheriff of Hereford.

Walter also held lands at Ludlow, Weobley and Ewyas Harold, and looked after William de Braose's estates in Ireland.

## Giles (c.1180–1215)
Appointed bishop of Hereford in 1200.

Giles had fled to Paris with Stephen Langdon, archbishop of Canterbury, during John's interregnum. He returned to England in 1213 and started to reclaim his father's Welsh estates from John, achieving some success before dying in November 1215. His brother Reginald continued the fight.

## John Knill or Knyll (c.1180–d. before 1205)
m. 1204 Amabil (Mabel) de Limesi, widow of Hugh Bardolf, the royal justiciar and sheriff.

As his inheritance, William gave John the manor of Knyll and thereafter he adopted the surname Knill. On John's death in 1205, William was released from the £1,000 fee he owed to King John for permission to allow his son to marry.[4]

## Reginald (1182– c.1228)
9th lord of Abergavenny
m. 1) Grecia de Briwere (c.1176–before 1215) born in Devon.
m. 2) Gwladus Ddu (the dark-eyed) (d.1251) the daughter of Llywelyn ab Iorwerth (the Great) and Joan, illegitimate daughter of King John. After Reginald's death she married Ralph Mortimer of Wigmore.

Reginald was successful in regaining most of the de Braose family estates, including Brecknock and Radnor. His son with Grecia was William v de Braose (1204–30) 10th baron of Abergavenny (also known as Black William). He married Eva, the daughter of the powerful knight William Marshal. Eva was responsible for raising a murage tax in 1237 to pay for the building of the town walls of Hay. William was hanged by Llywelyn ab Iorwerth (the Great) in 1230 after being caught in the chamber of his wife Joan (Jannet). This incident is the subject of the celebrated Welsh-language play Siwan by Saunders Lewis.

When William was executed in 1230, he had no sons. Accordingly, all his lands and titles were divided between his four daughters. Thus, the senior line of the powerful de Braose family ended abruptly and the lands dispersed to the families of their husbands (*see family tree on p. 13*). William had been at Llywelyn's court to finalise the arrangements for his daughter's marriage to Llywelyn's son, Dafydd. Despite William's execution, the marriage went ahead, with Isabella taking the lordship of Builth to her husband. Maud, whose share of the inheritance was Radnor, married Roger Mortimer of Wigmore (d.1282). Maud and her daughter-in-law built Kingsland Church, Herefordshire, between 1290–1300 and her arms are shown in the east window of the church. Eleanor inherited Brecknock (including Hay) and Kington which she took to her husband, Humphrey de Bohun, 2nd earl of Hereford. Finally, Eva married William III de Cantilupe, brother of St Thomas Cantilupe, bishop of Hereford, taking to her husband her inheritance of Abergavenny.

Annora (Eleanor) (*c.*1190–1241)[5]
m. (before 1210) Hugh Mortimer, heir of Ralph Mortimer of Wigmore.

Flandrina (*c.*1190–*c.*1248)
Abbess of Godstow nunnery 1242–48 (*see below*).

The children about whom there is considerable uncertainty although there exists circumstantial evidence to suggest they might possibly be Matilda's children:

Roger (b.*c*.1171–72)

Thomas (b.*c*.1175–76)

Henry (Hugh) (b.*c*.1180)
Very little is known about Henry but he may have been the Hugh named as a prebendary at Hereford Cathedral during Giles' time as bishop.

Philip (*c*.1190–*c*.1220)
m.1220 to Matilda (Eva) de Pont de l'Arche. On Philip's death Matilda married (c.1227) William fitz William, baron of Naas.

Bertha
m. William de Beauchamp (d.1197) of Elmley, Worcestershire, but details of this marriage are unclear and confusing.

Walter

Bernard (b.*c*.1197)

In addition, a number of other children have been attributed to Matilda and William, with some family trees claiming as many as 24 or more possible offspring for the couple. The provenance of these is suspect but two names appear relatively frequently, with an intriguing third possibility also cropping up:

Joane Avice (Alice) (*c*.1175–1215)
m. Richard de Percy, 5th Baron Percy, and one of the 25 named as enforcers of the Magna Carta.

There is a great deal of conjecture and confusion about Joane's parents but she was probably the daughter of Reginald de Braose, brother to William II.

Susan

Details about Susan are particularly confusing. She is shown on family trees as a descendant or sibling of various members of the family. Possibly this is because of a general supposition that she was also called Maud, or that Matilda's second child Maud had Susan as a second name. There are two supposed age ranges.

1) 1133–1201, which means that she was the daughter of William II and Bertha of Gloucester, and half-sister of William III.

2) 1173–1215, which suggests she could have been the second child of Matilda, who we know as Maud and not Susan, but the dates of death disagree.

Margery

An intriguing suggestion – that one of Matilda's elder children was called Margery, and that she may not be the daughter of William III de Braose – occurs in a manuscript showing the descendants of the founders of Llanthony Abbey. There is no other mention of Margery. It seems that this was a clerical error and a misnaming of one of Matilda's other children. No primary sources or other material exist to indicate that Matilda married twice, had a liaison with someone else or adopted a child. It may be that Margery was taken in by Matilda when some unfortunate event befell her birth parents, or this could be just another inaccuracy thrown up when trying to trace early history.

## Religious Convictions of Matilda's Children

It is impossible to tell how much direct influence William and Matilda's religious convictions had on their children, but we know that some displayed strong religious leanings.

The Church had a major influence on all aspects of life in the Middle Ages. It had great power and used it to influence the politics of the country and political appointments. There was also a religious element to most aspects of daily life. Matilda, even though she was the wife of an important baron, would have been as subject to the constraints imposed by its influence as anyone else in the country.

We do not know if Matilda and William displayed overt religious tendencies from an early age but Gerald of Wales described Matilda as having strong religious impulses, as did her husband. While this appears complimentary, again we do not really know if Gerald had an ulterior motive for his account.

William was brought up as a powerful Marcher lord and as such was required to give leadership and act in a strong and decisive fashion from an early age. In the Marches there were constant threats and rebellions by the local Welsh chieftains. To hold and enlarge his lands he had to act ruthlessly. Possibly, this went against his religious convictions. His conscience may have troubled him later when reflecting on his 'Ogre of Abergavenny' massacre (as previously discussed) of Christmas Day 1175. He may also have had later reservations about his violent pursuit of various Welsh princes, and wanted absolution for their murders.

In those days there was a general expectation that any family of influence might, for example, endow the founding of an abbey. The lord would support it financially in return for hospitality whenever he visited. He would also expect to be buried there with his wife, and have Masses said for their souls.

Records show that William greatly extended the church of St Mary de Haura at New Shoreham in Sussex, five years after the Abergavenny massacre. It is thought possible he intended to establish an abbey there. William also rebuilt or restored many churches in his lands including at Skenfrith, Grosmont, Brecknock and Abergavenny. Later in the 1190s William gave grants to the monks of Flaxley Abbey,[6] Gloucester so that they would pray for his soul and that of Matilda. He also gave the tithes of Llanfihangel Nant Melan in Radnorshire to the Knights of the Order of St John in Jerusalem.

In 1207/8, before they were outlawed, Matilda and William granted the churches of Hay, Talgarth, Llanigon and Llangorse, together with their chapels, tithes, woods and villeins, to St John's Priory, Brecknock. This was for the forgiveness of their sins and the sake of their souls and those of their descendants. Their largesse extended beyond the Marches as far as the abbey at Glastonbury in Somerset.

Matilda in her own right was one of the founders of Llanthony Prima Abbey, a few miles south of Hay, among the Black Mountains. It has been suggested that Matilda gave precious linen to St Edmund's Abbey, Bury St Edmunds, as one of her last acts before she died. Where this idea came from is unknown.[7] We also do not know to what extent Matilda acted independently, or how much she was influenced by her husband or others.

All these actions support Gerald's view that William, despite his fierce reputation, was also devout. Gerald records that whenever William spoke, he always invoked the name of the Lord before starting a sentence. William was also in the habit of overloading his letters with references that asked for God's indulgence. According to Gerald, if William saw a church, he would immediately break off what he was doing and pray, and when he rode through Brecknock, he exchanged God's blessing with the little children there. He is known to have been generous in his endowments to the priories of Abergavenny and Brecknock.

William is said to have wished to be buried in Brecknock Church because he loved it so much, and he had faith in St John after God and Mary.[8] It would be customary for Matilda to be buried with her husband. Unfortunately, due to the circumstances that unfolded, neither could be carried out.

## Giles de Braose

Giles was the second of Matilda's surviving sons and became bishop of Hereford. Nothing is known for certain about his early life but the design of his bishop's seal shows a tonsured cleric. This has led to conjecture that he may have been in holy orders, possibly as an archdeacon, and possibly in France.

Senior appointments in the realm, whether secular or religious, were largely political. They were in the gift of the king, and history shows that positions often went to royal favourites. It seems likely that William had an influence in his son's appointment as he was a supporter and close confidant of the king. Another factor in his appointment might have been that he was seen as a safe pair of hands in a dispute between the Hereford and Llandaff dioceses. Archenfield lay just over the border from Wales in Herefordshire, but was claimed by the Church of Wales. At one time the Welsh border lay further to the east and thus included it. Appointing Giles ensured that Archenfield remained in the English Church.

Giles was consecrated bishop on 24 September 1200 in St Catherine's chapel, Westminster.[9] At the beginning of John's reign Giles was in royal favour, no doubt influenced to some extent by John's support of William and Matilda. His estate was at Bishop's Castle in Shropshire.

Giles supported the king during his dispute with Pope Innocent III in Rome over the appointment of the archbishop of Canterbury. John wanted his own man and refused to recognise the Pope's appointment of Stephen Langton. As a result, the Pope imposed an interdict on England in 1208. At this, Giles and other bishops were forced to flee to France in May of that year.[10] Giles' lands were confiscated by the Crown and given to Gerard d'Athée to administer.

Matilda's second son, Giles de Braose, bishop of Hereford, commemorated in a window in Brecon Cathedral (© P. Ford)

While in France, Giles and the other exiled clerics, including Archbishop Stephen Langton, taught at the English college in Paris (where William exiled himself after his downfall). Eventually, John and Pope Innocent III made peace and on 16 July 1213 Giles returned. He resumed his previous position and, at least on paper, John agreed to return all the de Braose estates to the family and pay compensation.

When the king was slow in keeping to this agreement, Giles rebelled. Once again John confiscated his private lands. Giles then temporarily sided with Llywelyn ab Iorwerth and the other Marcher lords. Eventually, realising continued resistance was futile, they made peace with the king.

Still desperate to see the de Braose estates returned to the family, Giles and his brother Reginald fell out with John again during Llywelyn's rebellion of 1215. They seized their old family lands in the Marches, and after some prevarication John eventually allowed the brothers to retain them. Even so, John forced Giles to pay a fine of 9,000 marks to receive them back into his possession.

Just a few months later, Giles, bishop of Hereford and 5th baron of Bramber, was one of three bishops who joined the barons when they witnessed the agreeing of the Magna Carta. He was not one of the 25 barons who comprised the security council charged with enforcing the charter against the king. This was despite Giles being at the forefront in defying the king.

Possibly, the barons felt it was a military not a spiritual matter to ensure the charter was enforced. It could also have been because Giles was ill. He died shortly afterwards on 17 November 1215 and is buried in Hereford Cathedral.[11]

Giles built the tower at St John the Evangelist Church in Brecknock. This is now the cathedral, and where he has a commemorative window. Giles is also believed to have overseen the building of the central tower of Hereford Cathedral with its fine decorative work and ballflowers.[12]

Two other members of the extended de Braose family also had connections to Hereford Cathedral during Giles' tenure as bishop. One of Matilda's relatives, Henry de St Valery, was a witness to John's Charter of Liberties to Hereford Cathedral in 1203. Another relative, Hugh de Braose was a prebendary there.[13]

## Flandrina

Flandrina is a daughter of Matilda about whom we know very little. One account gives her date range as c.1190 to c.1248, but there is no indication of the source of this conjecture. She became a nun at Godstow nunnery, probably at an early age, and went on to be elected abbess in 1242. For some unknown reason, she was deposed in 1248 by the bishop of Lincoln.[14] Possibly she died at this time. The Godstow Cartulary[15] sheds no light on this incident.

## Anchoresses

In addition to Flandrina, three more of Matilda's daughters displayed strong religious tendencies, and may have been influenced by their experiences as outcasts and the manner of their mother's death. Loretta and Annora became anchoresses, and Margaret founded a church in memory of their mother.

Anchorites and anchoresses were a feature of religious life during the Middle Ages. The name comes from the Greek word anachoreo meaning 'to withdraw' or 'to retire'. They were a type of hermit, with a female to male ratio of up to four to one, who retired to a religious life. Anchorites vowed to remain in one place, and frequently were sealed in a cell built against the outside wall of a church or chapel. These were known as anchorholds. Anchorites would remain in their cells permanently but be able to participate in Masses through a small window or squint into the church. They were not subject to the rules of a religious house and were able to retain a measure of independence.

Due to their religious life, they provided a focus for people wishing to consult for advice or spiritual guidance. There is evidence that they were also able to exercise a degree of influence at some distance from their anchorholds. Frequently, there would be an adjoining room for a servant, sometimes two, who provided them with food and disposed of 'night soil' via a chamber pot.

The importance attached to such roles was demonstrated by the exchequer. Henry III paid a maintenance grant to 27 anchorites and anchoresses throughout his reign. Evidently, this was to ensure that they prayed for the king and earned him a place in heaven.

## Loretta

Loretta was the second eldest daughter of Matilda. She married (c.1196) Robert (fitz Parnell) de Beaumont, 4th earl of Leicester. In 1204 she became a widow when only in her late-20s after her husband was killed after campaigning in France for both Richard I and John.

Circumstantial evidence supports the notion that she had contemplated a religious retreat a few years after her husband's death. In 1207 John required her to agree not to remarry or become a nun for a year. Despite her husband's loyal service, this undertaking made life difficult for her shortly afterwards. She was a widow, her parents were outlawed and her brother Giles had to escape to France because of the interdict. When John seized her lands at around the time of the outlawing, Loretta escaped to France with her brother and father.

Eventually, she returned, probably with Giles when he came back in 1213. She agreed with John that she would not remarry without his permission. This allowed her to regain her father's old estates at Tawstock near Barnstable in Devon, and land in Dorset and Hampshire at the end of 1214. She leased these out in 1219, giving her an income, and possibly retained them until her death.

Loretta, possibly influenced by her brother Giles and Archbishop Stephen Langton, supported the Franciscans. She was instrumental, with Simon Langdon (brother of Archbishop Langton), in getting permission for the Franciscan order to establish their first priory in Canterbury. It has also been suggested that she influenced her sister Annora's husband Hugh Mortimer whose nephew became a Franciscan monk.[16] Her contact with her brother and the archbishop in France may have sown the seeds for her decision to become an anchoress. By 1221 she was enclosed at Hackington, just north of the shrine of St Thomas Becket at Canterbury. His shrine was dedicated in 1220 and rapidly became the most visited in the country. Being close by, Loretta would have had many visitors, often from Europe, when they passed on pilgrimage.

Because they had withdrawn into a life of religious contemplation, anchoresses were thought to be uncorrupted by the normal world. Consequently, they were often consulted for advice, and seclusion did not prevent them from participating in aspects of the outside world. Loretta was known to have continued her support of the Franciscans. Although a widow, and enclosed, there is a record by Thomas of Ecclestone that she welcomed the first friars to England when they visited Canterbury in 1224.[17]

Loretta remained relatively wealthy and was able to retain two female and, unusually, one male servant to support her. Using her influence, she enabled her male servant to be excused jury or assize duty.

Seemingly, he was kept busy as she often sent him off to intercede, very successfully, with the king or his officials on behalf of her neighbours.

The status of anchoresses was such that wealthy families often gave them patronage. Alice, lady of Hastings and Tickhill, sent two sides of bacon, two quarts of wheat and of barley, and one of oats, annually to her. When Alice died, Henry III continued to supply these as well as lamb, cheese and eggs.[18]

The last we hear of Loretta was when she received a letter in 1265 from Simon de Montfort, a distant relative. He was asking for her help regarding the stewardship of England, as related to the earls of Leicester. This was more than 60 years after her husband died. Loretta died in *c*.1266 aged approximately 89 years. Possibly it was Loretta's religious background and influence that induced her younger sister Annora to follow her lead and become an anchoress.[19]

## Annora

Annora became Lady Mortimer when she married Hugh Mortimer, heir to Roger Mortimer of Wigmore. She was with her mother Matilda when she fled to Ireland, and imprisoned with her mother at Bristol after they were all captured in Scotland trying to escape. After her mother and brother William IV were removed to Windsor and Corfe Castle, Annora continued to be held at Bristol. She was finally released three years later in 1214 when her husband inherited the title 4th Mortimer lord of Wigmore. He received her *maritagium* or marriage portion the following year. Unfortunately, Hugh died in 1227 as the result of an accident at a tournament, and they had no children.

This made Annora a widow in her 30s, but she does not appear to have been such a desirable catch as Loretta when she was widowed. Accounts indicate that she led a solitary existence for a time, perhaps conscious that she was not being made particularly welcome by her brother-in-law who had inherited the Mortimer title. In 1232 Annora received permission to reserve 100 shillings from her marriage portion for expenses, as long as she remained a recluse. This has been taken to mean that this is when she became an anchoress, at Iffley (also in Oxfordshire).

Why Iffley? We may never know for sure, but Iffley was around seven miles away (well within a day's walk) from Godstow Priory. During her married life, Annora had been a patroness to Godstow where her sister Flandrina was a nun. Godstow had a history of support by the de Braose family, and the St Valery estates were nearby. Godstow was important as it was the place where Henry II's mistress 'Fair' Rosamund Clifford was buried. There is documentary evidence that while anchorites and anchoresses may have been confined in one place, they were often in contact with one another. Their servants would convey messages back and forth. Thus, Iffley was well-placed for messages to Godstow, or other anchorites nearby.

Annora is now known as The Recluse of St Mary's Church at Iffley.[20] She has become famous through the references to her in the Rolls of Henry III. He granted her oaks from the Shotover forest, a sack of grain, a robe and timbers for building. These alms ceased in 1241, so this may be around the time that she died.

## Margaret

Matilda's eldest daughter Margaret de Lacy wanted to ensure that her mother was remembered. Five years after Matilda's death, she obtained John's permission to dedicate a chapel to the memory of her mother, father and brother.[21] In letters patent issued on 10 October 1216, eight days before his death, John granted Margaret three carucates of land in the forest of Aconbury. This was to build not just a chapel but also a religious house (in other words, a priory). A carucate was the medieval unit of land a plough team of eight oxen could till in a single annual season, or about 120 acres. The gift is the last item recorded on John's Patent Roll and it was sent to Walter de Lacy of Ludlow Castle, but to be assigned to his wife Margaret, Matilda's daughter. Walter was sheriff of Hereford and an executor of John's will so it is possibly due to his influence that the grant was given.

The Hospital of St John in the royal forest at Aconbury near Holme Lacy in Herefordshire was founded in 1218. Despite being under the military order of St John it was set up as a women's house to pray for the souls of Matilda, her husband and son. Monks would travel to it for Mass and the giving of the sacrament. More than a century later Matilda's grandson, John de Braose, bestowed the income from a row of cottages in Tetbury on the nunnery.

We know that by 1233 Margaret had issues with the Hospitallers over their rule at Aconbury. She was in dispute with them for a number of years and during that time there was no appointed prioress. Margaret fulfilled the role of sub-prioress until the chapel was transferred to the Rule of St Augustine in 1237.

Margaret's husband Walter de Lacy died in 1241. Traditionally, this was the occasion for widows to retire to a religious house, but Margaret does not seem to have done that. Despite her founding and support of the priory, there is no indication that she became a nun or retired to Aconbury before she died on 17 November 1255. Margaret is buried in the Priory Church, Holme Lacy, next to her husband. Although Aconbury Priory was founded to remember them, any attempt to identify where Matilda and her son William IV were buried, so long after their deaths, is conjecture. Given the manner of their deaths, it seems unlikely that their bodies were returned to their family at the time.

Nevertheless, there is speculation that William IV may have been buried at Sele Priory, Upper Beeding in West Sussex. While the priory had been founded before the Conquest, in 1126 it received generous grants from William I de Braose, the 1st lord of Bramber. It continued to be supported by the de Braose family for many years.

Aconbury church still exists, although the nunnery buildings were demolished in the nineteenth century when a house was built on the site. In the south wall of the church is a square squint thought to have been used by the prioress. Could this squint have been used by Margaret when she acted as sub-prioress before the appointment of a permanent prioress? We will never know. Unfortunately, the church is now closed and only used as a store by the Hereford Deanery.

## Ancrene Wisse

A well-known document, the revised Ancrene Wisse or Anchoresses Guide, was published sometime around 1240. This was a revision of earlier documents originally written for three sisters of noble birth in the Welsh Marches who became anchoresses. If Margaret had been the third sister to become an anchoress, this might have suggested that this famous document was written for the three daughters of Matilda. However, we know this was not the case as the original Ancrene Wisse was written for sisters who became anchoresses as young women.

The revised document does, however, contain clauses that were designed specifically to make life easier for widows. As such, it would have been of use to the de Braose sisters who chose to become anchoresses. Traditionally, widows retreated to a nunnery as the preferred way to avoid pressure from the king to remarry someone not of their choice. A more attractive alternative to ladies who wanted to maintain a degree of independence, outside the constraints of a religious house, was to become an anchoress.

It has been suggested that the reason why the very early, original copy of this text was found at Wigmore Abbey may be because it was written by a monk there. Maud de Clare, granddaughter of Matilda's son William IV, also possessed a copy. (For a detailed and highly recommended explanation of the Ancrene Wisse and the de Braose connection, see the paper by Catherine Innes-Parker.[22])

# CHAPTER 5

# Magna Carta and the Legacies of Matilda

F OR centuries there has been conjecture that the death of Matilda gave rise to the writing of one of the most famous clauses in the Magna Carta, one that is still enshrined in British law – clause 39.

The Magna Carta came about as a result of the unrest between the English barons and King John. This had been building for years, and resulted in a number of minor revolts amid growing discontent within the country. There were a number of reasons for this unrest, but largely it was triggered by the actions of the king. John was a cruel, spiteful and avaricious man. His excessive demands for money, and his destruction of his staunch supporter William de Braose, despite all his loyal service, made the barons feel increasingly insecure; and John's brutal murder of a lady by starvation was viewed as being particularly abhorrent.

## Unknown Charter

In early 1215, with the discontent finally coming to a head, the barons drafted the 'Unknown Charter' in an attempt to address their core concerns. While this was only a rough draft, much of the content was redrafted and became incorporated into the Magna Carta itself.

The Unknown Charter started with a restatement of the Charter of Liberties granted by Henry I in 1100 on his accession to the throne. This set out principles of good government of the people, fair taxes, and civil liberties based on the laws of Edward the Confessor. This was followed by a set of draft clauses. These were a combination of specific limits on the ability of the king to abuse his power, and broad statements about the principles of good treatment of the population by their monarch. It required the king to act fairly, and not to seek excessive taxes. This addressed the concerns of barons whom John had personally slighted, but also those with a broader view of the principles of good Christian government.

Importantly, these clauses were prefaced by a far-reaching statement: 'King John concedes that he will arrest no man without judgement nor accept any payment for justice nor commit any unjust act'.[1] While this statement went on to be re-worded, it shows the principles the barons had in mind from the outset. Not all of the ideas in the charter went on to be part of the Magna Carta itself (for example, limiting scutage, the tax paid in lieu of knights service, and removal of an obligation of the barons to obey the king's summons to wage war in parts of France).

The charter was discussed at a series of meetings between John and the barons, but John refused to accept the principles enshrined in it. Exasperated, he declared war on the disaffected barons and laid siege to their castles. Opinion among the barons about what to do next was divided. Many of them continued to support the king but John could see the level of rebellion, which included the taking of London by a rebel force, so he agreed to further negotiations.

The Unknown Charter is so-called because it was only discovered in the French National Archives in 1863, and not made public until the 1890s. There is speculation that it was taken to France in 1215, possibly by Simon Langton who was an employee of the French court.[2]

## Articles of the Barons

A second draft document was subsequently produced: the Articles of the Barons. This reworked the wording of the Unknown Charter and gives a good demonstration on how the initial ideas evolved into a practical document listing the barons' demands.

At the public meetings to discuss and negotiate the various clauses in this document, John behaved civilly to the barons. However, Matthew Paris probably summed up his feelings when he reported that the king 'gnashed his teeth' and 'rolled his eyes', pacing around angrily in the privacy of the royal apartments afterwards. He was not happy with how discussions were going but realised that the simmering level of rebellion meant he had no choice but to appear to take it seriously.

Eventually, the articles were agreed by John as they bear his official seal, and are thought to date to 10 June.

## Magna Carta 1215

It was only a few days after the Articles were agreed that both parties came together in a final document – what we now call the Magna Carta or Great Charter. The charter records that it was agreed on 15 June 1215 in 'the meadow which is called Runnymede, between Windsor and Staines' by the River Thames.

Despite the wording of the document, historians are still debating whether it was really agreed on 19 June and not the 15 June, and how many alterations were made to it shortly afterwards. (All this is clearly explained by David Carpenter in his excellent book entitled simply *Magna Carta*.[3]) Importantly, however, a compromise had been reached and a set of principles agreed.

The charter is a curious document to have become the foundation of British constitutional history. In many ways it can be seen as a peace treaty between the barons and John, and a protector of the baronial rights. It was an attempt to restrict the power of the monarchy and make the king subject to the rule of law. There was little in it for the unfree peasants who formed the bulk of the population, or women, or even the knight class who owed their allegiance to the barons. The famous clauses 39 and 40, restricting the king's right to act arbitrarily, only applied to freemen. These were the minority in 1215. There is little to suggest there was any intention that it would be a bill of rights for the majority of the populace, as generally perceived today.

Primarily, the Magna Carta concentrated on financial aspects of the king's rule – not just taxation but also the arbitrary imposition of fines, or confiscation of estates requiring the holders to pay the king to get them back. This was perhaps an indication of the barons' priorities due to the financial pressure put on them, first by Henry II, then Richard I, but particularly by John. After all, it was a financial issue – William's huge debts – that the barons were told was the reason for John's actions against William and Matilda. Many of the barons were aware they too owed the exchequer considerable sums.

Secondly, it addressed grievances about administrative matters and fairness. There were clauses covering universal justice and treatment of the individual – 'the common good'. Attempts were made to restrict the king's powers to appoint unsuitable officials, and to be able to remove them from office if they were found to be corrupt. There were also attempts to restrict the king from deciding who could marry whom, and asserting the right of a widow to choose not to remarry.

Unsurprisingly, the whole charter is directed largely towards men, women having little meaningful place in medieval public life. Forty men are named individually in the charter, and collectively 'men' are mentioned 19 times. In contrast, the term 'woman' appears only once, and the term 'widows' appears in four clauses. It is probable that the rights of women were intended to be covered in the clauses which referred generically to mankind.

## Clause 39

The most famous clause in the 1215 charter is clause 39, followed closely by clause 40. They both refer to mankind in general, but clause 39 can be interpreted to relate directly to John's treatment of Matilda. Speculation has always been that it was instigated by her death. The original Latin clause 39 in the charter reads:

*Nullus liber homo capiatur, vel inprisonetur, aut dissaisiatur, aut utlagetur, aut exuletur, aut aliquo modo destruatur, nec super eum ibimus, nec super eum mittemus, nisi per legale judicium parium suorum vel per legem terrae.*[4]

A direct translation of this is:

No free man will be taken or imprisoned or disseised or outlawed or exiled or in any way ruined, nor will we go or send against him, save by the lawful judgement of his peers and by the law of the land.

A modern interpretation can be read as:

No man shall be taken, imprisoned, outlawed, banished or in
any way destroyed, nor will we proceed against or persecute him,
except by the lawful judgement of his peers and by the law of the
land.

This clause embodies two fundamental principles: 1) The right to personal freedom, and: 2) The rule of law.

John was renowned for seizing the property of those he had fallen
out with. Clause 39 was an attempt to curb his habit of making arbitrary
judgements against those with whom he had a dispute, did not trust
or were seen as inconvenient to the Crown. The Court Rolls record a
number of instances of this, such as when John suspected Ranulf of
Chester of having dealings with the Welsh prince Gwenwynwyn, so
seized his lands. Similarly, Roger of Montbegon suffered the same fate
when he failed to obey a summons to court. With no specific evidence
to distrust William, John not only had him and Matilda outlawed,
but also seized the lands of most of the rest of their family, including
Loretta, Giles and Reginald.

Curiously, clause 39 is the only one to refer to crime, albeit obliquely
when it refers to 'outlawed'. Many of the disputes between kings and
their barons involved criminal acts of some sort, and yet this was
almost ignored in the clause. The clause was also heavily male-orien-
tated. Only men could be outlawed. Women were 'waived', effectively
treated as a waif (as one abandoned, who could be killed on sight).

Despite the justifiable fame of clause 39 for its good intentions, it is
not difficult to identify issues with the practicalities of the wording.
Who were the 'peers' it refers to? What is 'lawful judgement'? And
what even was 'the law of the land', given that the law itself was still
vague in many areas? Nevertheless, the clause was used at least once
by a woman. Isabell, the countess of Lincoln, claimed Henry III had
broken the clause in his dealings with her.[5]

Over time, this clause has been claimed to enshrine trial by jury,
*Habeas Corpus*, and the need for justice to overbear the power of the

government. This it manifestly fails to do, but it alludes to elements of a fair justice system that was already in existence.

Henry II had introduced a system whereby judges made circuits of the country to provide timely justice, rather than wait for the king's presence and convenience, to resolve legal matters. The judges formed a jury of 12 local people to decide guilt or innocence. Subsequently, this system collapsed. In John's time, criminality was usually decided by trial by ordeal or combat, not by a jury. *Habeas Corpus* was not enshrined in law until the Act of 1679. However, whatever the practicalities of the clause, its intentions were laudable. It represented an attempt to curb the arbitrary nature of royal decision-making.

Whatever John's real views, he eventually acknowledged his assent to the charter. None of the copies bear John's signature, but he allowed his great seal to be attached to them. Affixing the seal was a specialist role carried out by a clerk known as a *spigurnel*, and this sealing would have been done to each of a number of copies that were then sent around the kingdom. Whether this was actually carried out at Runnymede is doubtful.

Did the Magna Carta achieve its aims and intentions? Not initially at least. John certainly ignored the charter, and within nine weeks it was formally rejected by both him and the Pope.

Nevertheless, the principles of the charter did not die. Henry III reissued it as his Coronation Charter in 1216, albeit with many of the parochial administrative clauses related to John's reign omitted. These were the clauses the barons had inserted in order to create more of a peace treaty with John than a charter of rights. This later version went on to be revised and reissued again and again. These were the Magna Cartas of 1217, 1225, 1234, 1265, 1297 and 1300. It is Henry III's 1225 version that has carried the most sway over time. The original clauses were slimmed down from 63 to 37, meaning that clause 39 thus became clause 29.

All the reissues were carried out by the reigning king to confirm his intention to uphold the ideals of the charter, but they were sealed by the king's ministers rather than the royal seal. This was important as it meant that it was no longer revocable by the king on a whim.

As the thirteenth century wore on, the charter became more widely circulated. Initially written only in Latin, it was later translated into baronial French, and English for the common people. Copies were issued throughout the realm, and some crossed the Channel to appear in France and elsewhere.

The charter has gone on to achieve an importance greatly exceeding that originally envisaged by the barons when they drew it up. In particular, clause 39 has enshrined fundamental rights that have been adopted by nations across the world. For generations, people in numerous countries have used the concepts behind clause 39 to foster freedom and justice.

The Fifth Amendment of the American Constitution asserts that 'No free man is to be arrested, or imprisoned, or disseized, or outlawed, or exiled, or in any other way ruined, nor will we go or send against him, except by the legal judgement of his peers or by the law of the land.' Similar wording has been incorporated into the constitutions of many of the individual states of America. In France, the Declaration of Rights of Man and Citizen 1789 is part of the French Constitution. Article 7 states that no person 'shall be accused, arrested, or imprisoned except in the cases and according to the forms prescribed by law.'

The wording, brought up to date, is used in the Universal Declaration of Human Rights (General Assembly resolution 217A) proclaimed by the United Nations General Assembly in Paris on 10 December 1948. Article 9 says 'No one shall be subjected to arbitrary arrest, detention or exile.' Again, the European Human Rights Act 1998 in article 5, the Right of Liberty, states 'No one shall be deprived of his liberty save …. in accordance with a procedure prescribed by law.'

This principle of 'the rule of law' was present in the constitutions of many of the states of Europe. The European Union formally codified it in their Charter of Fundamental Rights proclaimed in 2000. Article 52 reads 'any limitation on the exercise of the rights and freedoms recognised by this Charter must be provided for by law.'

In its home country, clause 39 is one of only four (or more accurately three and a half) that were not replaced by new legislation in 1970. The clauses still enshrined in English law are:

Clause 1    *The liberties of the English Church*
Clause 13    *The privileges of the City of London*
Clauses 39/40    *The rule of law*

For Matilda, what more fitting epitaph could there be than this famous clause. A woman who was one of the most powerful of her age, but who was treated so abominably at the end. A small consolation to Matilda would have been to see her son Giles, bishop of Hereford, among the barons pressurising John at Runnymede. She might also have noticed among the throng her grandson John de Braose, the son of William IV, who had died with her so tragically at Corfe Castle.

## Matilda and the Monarchy

A second legacy of Matilda is her contribution to the dynastic heritage of the British monarchy. Through her direct line, it is possible to demonstrate that after a number of generations her descendants united with those of King John:

**Matilda de St Valery** m. William III de Braose
↓
son Reginald de Braose m. Gwladus Ddu
↓
son William V de Braose m. Eva Marshal,
baroness of Abergavenny and daughter of Sir William Marshal
↓
daughter Eleanor de Braose m. Humphrey V de Bohun
2nd earl of Hereford
↓
son Humphrey VI de Bohun, 3rd earl of Hereford m. Maud de Fiennes
↓
son Humphrey VII de Bohun, 4th earl of Hereford m. Elizabeth of Rhuddlan,
daughter of Edward I and Eleanor of Castile
↓
son William de Bohun, 1st earl of Northampton m. Elizabeth of Badlesmere
↓
son Humphrey IX de Bohun, 7th earl of Hereford m. Joan Fitzalan
↓
daughter Mary de Bohun m. **Henry Bolingbroke (Henry IV)**

King John m. Isabella of Angoulême
↓
son Henry III m. Eleanor of Provence
↓
son Edward I m. Eleanor of Castile
↓
daughter Elizabeth of Rhuddlan m. Humphrey VII de Bohun
↓
son William de Bohun, Ist earl of Northampton m. Elizabeth of Badlesmere
↓
son Humphrey IX de Bohun, 7th earl of Hereford m. Joan Fitzalan
↓
daughter Mary de Bohun m. **Henry Bolingbroke (Henry IV)**

The abbreviated lineages show how William de Bohun was a direct descendant of both Matilda and John. William's descendant, Mary de Bohun, married another descendant of King John, Henry Bolingbroke who later became Henry IV. Their son Henry V is a direct descendant of both family lines.

## The Legends of Matilda

Despite the limited information about aspects of her life, Matilda has achieved a form of immortality in her legacy of the legends that have arisen around her. Some of these can be directly related to incidents in her life, others from her profile as the wife of a powerful Marcher lord.

LEGEND ONE

*The downfall of William and Matilda was due to Matilda's remarks about King John and the death of Arthur of Brittany.* Traditionally, the fall of William III de Braose has been blamed on Matilda's lack of diplomacy in accusing John of being responsible for the disappearance of his nephew, Arthur of Brittany.[6]

BASIS FOR THE LEGEND

Matilda's outburst accusing John of failing to look after his nephew 'as he ought' was made to the king's messengers when they went to request the presence of William IV at court. He was to be a hostage to guarantee that his father, William III, would pay all the money he owed to the king. By 1208, this is believed to have amounted to around £50,000, which was equal to the whole of the exchequer income for a year. By this time, the disappearance of Arthur, and John's involvement, was an open secret. As early as 1204 he had been asked to produce Arthur's body, and when that did not happen people had come to their own conclusions. John would have been aware of people's suspicions, so his reaction to Matilda's comments by outlawing the de Braoses may have had an element of posturing.[7]

Matilda's comment was made very publicly, and word would have spread quickly to all the other nobles. The king's troubled relationship with his barons meant he had to counter this defiance decisively. John's initial reaction to the accusation was probably genuine anger, which he made public for all to see. It is also possible, somewhat uncharacteristically, that it could have awakened a guilty conscience in him.

CONCLUSION

Whatever the true reason,[8] John was able to use Matilda's statement to create a smokescreen for the removal of an important and powerful baron whose loyalty he may have begun to distrust. It allowed him to justify his vendetta without making the true reason public, and also served as a warning to other barons not to cross their monarch. This incident led ultimately to the tragic death of Matilda and her eldest son.

Legend Two

*Matilda (as Moll Walbee) built Hay Castle in one night.*[9] Matilda had the reputation amongst the Welsh of being the giantess Moll Walbee, and of using occult powers to build Hay Castle in a single night carrying the stones in her apron.[10]

BASIS FOR THE LEGEND

The early history of Hay, from the time of the Conquest until 1200, is imprecise. It is known that Sir Philip Walwyn, one of Bernard de Neufmarché's knights, built a motte and bailey castle at Hay. It is assumed this was the one by St Mary's Church outside the town walls, in the area once known as Weston. This simple stronghold was never developed into a stone castle.

Sir William Revell is also said to have built a castle at Hay. As discussed earlier, it is possible that it was a second motte and bailey castle, or that he built or inherited the stone gatehouse tower currently referred to as the keep on the existing main castle site. By the time Matilda based herself in Hay, this had certainly been built. No evidence of any other stone building dating from that time has been found on the site.

Conflict and disorder between the Normans and the Welsh was a feature of everyday life in the Marches. Matilda led a successful defence of Painscastle in 1198. While the Welsh were defeated, this was the third such attack in a decade and may have led her to realise it would be wise to increase the defences at Hay. It is believed that shortly afterwards, around 1200, Matilda instigated the building of a new, bigger gateway next to the keep. This was complemented by removing the doors and blocking the archways in the gatehouse tower. A curtain wall was also built to encircle the castle site. This would appear to be the source of legend.

CONCLUSION
If the new stone gateway and curtain walls were built with a degree of urgency the castle walls may have seemed to appear almost overnight above the tree-line. This impression would have been enhanced if the walls were limewashed a gleaming white.

LEGEND THREE
*Moll Walbee threw a stone from her clog across the River Wye into Llowes churchyard.*[11] While Moll Walbee was building Hay Castle, legend has it that a stone fell from her apron into her clog. She was so annoyed she picked it up and threw it across the River Wye to land in Llowes churchyard, almost four miles away.[12]

Llowes Church is dedicated to St Meilig or Maelog, a sixth-century saint, brother to St Gildas and son of a Scottish chieftain, Caw from Strathclyde. In the church is a large standing slab cross known as St Meilig's Cross (*see p. 91*). There is a great deal of speculation about its history. Originally the cross was thought to date from the sixth century due to the crude cross carved on one side. More recently, however, suggestions have been made that it is probably tenth- to twelfth-century, based on when the more decorative cross on the other side was carved. Some scholars have even made the suggestion that it was originally a Bronze Age menhir or standing stone, subsequently remodelled.

Whatever its origin, local tradition holds that the stone stood in the hills above Llowes at Croesfeilliog, Welsh for St Meilig's Cross. It stood where the parishes of Llowes, Clyro and Llanddewi Fach meet.[13] St Meilig is said to have carved the scratch dial on the side which shows the hours of the day. There is dispute about whether there may even have been a wooden cross or possibly a pagan standing stone at the site originally. A number of alternative original locations have tentatively been suggested, including Bryn Rhydd Common and Llowes Common, both a short distance from the church.[14] Whatever the stone's origin, it was moved in the twelfth century to the churchyard.

### WECHELEN THE HERMIT OF LLOWES

The only possible connection with Matilda would appear to be that this stone was moved into the churchyard at Llowes during her lifetime, sometime around 1200–5, with their being no other obvious reason how it became known as Moll Walbee's Stone.

We cannot know why the stone was moved but it may have been to use it as a grave marker for Wechelen, the anchorite hermit of Llowes.[15] What we know of Wechelen has come from Gerald of Wales, who described Wechelen as a saint. We do not know exactly where Wechelen's cell was, but he describes hearing the priest saying Mass through his window. The priest also visited the cell to read the Gospels to Wechelen, so it must have been close to

The St Meilig's Cross, which now stands inside the church of St Meilig, Llowes. Once thought to date from the sixth century, it is now thought more likely that it dates from the tenth to the twelfth century (© P. Ford)

the church. Gerald went to Wechelen to obtain his blessing and
converse on a number of occasions as he was impressed by visions
Wechelen described. The old hermit was revered locally and people
would come to his window to touch his hand as they believed
he had healing powers. Wechelen was troubled by this, and the
Cistercian monks working the nearby farms belonging to Strata
Florida Abbey, such as Cabalva, Tir y Mynuch and Clyro Court,
tried to dissuade him from this. Wechelen discussed the issue with
Gerald who encouraged him to continue to use the healing power
that God had given him. The two of them conversed in Latin and
when Gerald enquired how Wechelen had come to acquire Latin
he replied that it was in Jerusalem and that he had visited the Holy
Sepulchre. The Second Crusade was in 1147 and it is just possible
that Wechelen may have joined this. Those on this crusade were
normally powerful, monied men not paupers, and although Gerald
describes Wechelen as a poor old man, Gerald also records him as
having a servant.

Matilda is thought to have enlisted the help of Wechelen to give
confidence and encouragement to her army when she advanced
over the Radnorshire hills into Wales in her conquest of Elfael.
The story goes that Matilda appeared before her ill-prepared and
unconfident English army disguised as a nun. Accompanying
her was a Welsh hermit from Llowes. It seems likely that this
was Wechelen as we know he was living at this time. Like many
hermits, he was revered as having almost saint-like qualities.[16] 'He
encouraged the men to go into battle without fear, which they did,
and killed three thousand of the enemy.' This story carries echoes
of Matilda's defence of Painscastle.

Wechelen mentions that he ate a small loaf of white bread
following one of his visions. This would have been unusual as
the Welsh, like the majority of poor people, tended to subsist on
cheaper rye bread.[17] Wheat was expensive. It was hard to grow
in the poor soils of Welsh hills, and mostly eaten by the richer
Normans who imported it from England. Where would Wechelen
obtain his supply? Either he was not as poor as Gerald portrays

him or Matilda may have given it in recognition of his past service to her. Hermits, like anchorites, were widely supported with alms from the wealthy, as previously discussed.

### AN ALTERNATIVE VERSION OF THE LEGEND

*There is an older version of the legend recorded in Radnorshire in which Moll Walbec – or Malaen-y-Walfa as she was also known – threw the stone from Clifford Castle.*

This earlier version of the legend, linking the stone to Clifford, involves a dispute between Sir Ralph Baskerville and Lord Clifford over the limits of their respective estates. Baskerville accused Clifford of appropriating his land and challenged him to single combat in order to settle the matter. While initial tales suggested that this occurred near Hereford, later stories placed it at White Cross at the junction of the Hereford road to Hay and Weobley. Later, it was concluded that any combat was more likely to have been at the border between the respective estates, on neutral ground such as at Llowes.

Regardless of where it happened, Baskerville was successful in the duel and killed Clifford. One version has the duel taking place in the churchyard, and for this Baskerville obtained a pardon from the Pope. This was not for killing Clifford but for fighting in a churchyard, 'an act of the most enormous profanity!'[18] The suggestion is that the stone was thrown into the churchyard of Llowes from the castle at Clifford, as a penance for Baskerville's actions. Chroniclers suggested the matter is beyond doubt because the stone bears the sculptured cross of the arms of Clifford. This version of the legend made little reference to Matilda when it was recorded in 1905. Since then, it seems to have been forgotten and the Hay Castle connection has taken precedence.[19]

### CONCLUSION

The second legend appears to have no credibility. As for the first legend, if we were to assume that Wechelen went on the Second Crusade this would make him around 70 to 75 years of age in 1200.

On this basis it is quite feasible that the cross was placed in the churchyard at around that time to mark the burial place of such a revered old hermit.

ADDENDUM

Today the cross only survives due to chance. A Mr Ernest Hartland, writing around 1873, said that the old parish clerk had told him of an incident that occurred when he was a boy. The late vicar stopped two men who were trying to dig up the cross. They intended to use it as the cornerstone for the new school, but after making a hole 4 feet (1.2m) deep they still had not reached the base. The vicar stopped them, ensured the hole was filled in, and sent the men on their way, so saving the cross for posterity.[20] The school was built in 1830. In November 1956 the stone was moved into the church itself to prevent further erosion.

CADW, the Welsh Government's historic environmental service, views St Meilig's Cross to be one of the finest standing slab-crosses in Wales. The rectangular stone is carved on both faces with Celtic-type Latin crosses. On one side the relatively crude carving has been dated to the sixth or seventh century, and the finer cross on the other side to the eleventh century. Current opinion, however, favours a common twelfth-century origin. When it was moved in 1956, it was found to be 12 feet (3.6 metres) in height, weighing approximately three tons and tapered at the base into a wedge shape. It has been reset lower into the ground than its original position. Shelves on two sides for candles or offerings were seen in 1690 by Edward Lhuyd, the linguist, antiquarian and botanist, but are now buried.[21] Curiously, the limestone of which it is made is not found in the locality, and the only other similar cross is in Durham Cathedral.

Legend Four

*Matilda's purse of emeralds.* For centuries there has been a persistent rumour that Matilda hid a purse of emeralds somewhere within Hay Castle to prevent King John getting hold of them.

As already described, William owed John a great deal of money. He was outlawed, with Matilda, after she publicly refused to allow her son William IV to go to court where he would have been held as a hostage against the repayment of the debt. Legend has it that John's second wife Isabella of Angoulême approached Matilda with a proposition. If Matilda would give John the purse of emeralds that she was believed to have, he would forget the episode. Matilda refused, supposedly hiding the stones somewhere in the castle, and the rest is history. We do not know if the emeralds existed, even though, given Matilda's status, it is highly likely that she would have had a number of precious gems. There is also conjecture that she hid money and gems in the Radnorshire hills, but again this is impossible to substantiate.

An alternative suggestion has been made that emeralds were hidden in the castle during the English Civil War of 1642–51. Herefordshire had a strong tradition of Royalist support, which would have included Hay. To protect their valuables from the Cromwellian forces, Royalists would endeavour to hide anything of value. While this is a more plausible origin of the emerald story, no direct evidence for it has been found.

CONCLUSION

Much of Matilda's original castle has been demolished over the centuries. It is believed that the chapel and Great Hall were demolished to build the Jacobean mansion. Only scant remains are left of the curtain wall, and a drawbridge and gatehouse mentioned in later accounts are no longer in existence. The mansion was built 400 years after Matilda's time. This had a major rebuild in 1910 by W.D. Caroe, as well as suffering two devastating fires subsequently. After all this time, even if they once existed, it is unlikely that any trace of a purse or emeralds would have survived intact. The legend is likely to be pure fantasy.

The front elevation of the Jacobean mansion built in 1640. This post-Second World War photograph shows the keep on the left, and shows the extensive nature of the rebuilding of the castle, together with the results of the fire in 1939, which gutted the left-hand portion of the mansion

LEGEND FIVE

*The effigy in St Mary's Church, Hay.* On 21 May 1804, Sir Richard Colt Hoare visited Hay. With him was the diarist Richard Fenton. Fenton recorded the local legend that an effigy in St Mary's Church in Hay depicted Moll Walbee.

BASIS FOR THE LEGEND

At the back of St Mary's Church is a stone effigy consisting of the head, torso and upper legs of a figure. It has suffered extensive erosion by the weather. No-one appears to know the origin of the effigy but it certainly predates the church which was rebuilt in 1832. While detail is poor due to the weathering, it is possible to make out that the hairstyle, the build of the torso and the style of the clothing are in keeping with a knight. As a consequence, the legend has always been dismissed. On the other hand, tradition has always said that Matilda wore armour when leading her army in Elfael. Might she also have had a cropped hairstyle?

In reality it is unlikely that this figure represents Matilda:

1. The appearance of the effigy works against it. Effigies of high-status women generally show them in a fine gown with appropriate accessories and headdress of the period.

2. Given the circumstances, King John is unlikely to have allowed Matilda's body to be returned to Hay.

3. If Matilda's body had been returned, her children would have ensured she had a tomb befitting of the lady of the manor, within the church. Even allowing for the rebuild, it is unlikely that such a tomb would have been removed. It could have been re-sited, either within the church or in the churchyard, but there is no evidence it ever existed.

4. King John gave permission for Matilda's daughter, Margaret, to found a chapel at Aconbury in memory of her mother. If the body was returned, it is more likely that it would have been buried there, away from Hay, and with a suitable memorial tomb. No record of one has ever been found.

Another effigy associated with the de Braose family does exist. William granted a charter to Tetbury for a market, and as a result it rapidly became a busy wool market. In gratitude, William was honoured with a monument in the church of St Mary the Virgin, Tetbury. The monument was buried when the church was rebuilt. Recently, a statue with a badly eroded head and torso was uncovered and placed near the chancel. Current thinking is that this is not William but Peter de Braose, a later descendant who lived in Tetbury.

LEGEND SIX

*Matilda was a lady-in-waiting to Queen Eleanor.* It has been suggested that Matilda may have been a lady-in-waiting to Queen Eleanor of Aquitaine, the wife of Henry II.

Ladies-in-waiting were important individuals drawn from the nobility. Their role included to support the queen on state occasions. The ladies of the privy chamber, on the other hand, were married women who became close confidantes of the queen. The queen's daily companions would be maids of honour. These were typically young girls of about 12 years of age, who came to court to complete their education, and most importantly to obtain a 'good marriage'.[22]

CIRCUMSTANTIAL EVIDENCE

Matilda was born around 1155 and married around 1166/ 69 when she was about 12 to 14 years old. At this time, Queen Eleanor would have been around 46 years of age. Her marriage to Henry had become strained and she was unhappy with Henry's treatment of her sons. He was unwilling to grant them estates and responsibilities of their own and she was sympathetic to their cause.[23] In 1168, Eleanor made the decision to base herself in France and support her favourite son Richard, whom she saw as the heir to her Province of Aquitaine. For the next ten years she mainly lived at her favourite castles and abbeys of Fontevrault, Poitiers, Argentan and Chinon. Visits to England were very infrequent and usually of limited duration. Around 1180, her sons rebelled against their father and Eleanor supported them. King Henry quelled the rebellion and forgave his sons but kept Eleanor imprisoned for the rest of his reign.[24]

It is possible that Matilda may have been a maid of honour for a time, but she would have been unmarried and too young to be a lady-in-waiting. Matilda was married about the time Eleanor retired to France and so she would have been occupied with households of her own. These would have been on William's estates, mainly based either at Bramber in Sussex or in the Marcher lands. It is unlikely that she visited France.

CONCLUSION

We do not know how regimented the system for choosing the queen's companions was in these early days before the Tudor courts. It is possible that Matilda attended court at Winchester or London shortly after her marriage. However, given the age gap and the queen's background, it seems unlikely that a young girl like Matilda would have achieved sufficient importance to become a lady-in-waiting in these early years.

After his sons' rebellion in 1170, Eleanor was confined by the king and only allowed a small number of ladies-in-waiting. When Matilda was older, given the toxic atmosphere that probably existed in her court, Eleanor would not have trusted anyone whom the king had chosen to attend her. After Henry died and Eleanor was released, she was an old woman and confined herself to France. By this time Matilda was ensconced in Hay. It is possible that Matilda was in attendance during Eleanor's infrequent visits to England, but in all probability Eleanor would have brought one of her regular French ladies with her.

A plausible explanation for the legend is that Matilda de Braose was mixed up with Mathilda of England, Queen Eleanor's eldest daughter. She accompanied her mother, and Eleanor also stayed with her, for the ten years after her sons' rebellion.

There are other less likely possibilities. William's aunt – his father's sister – was called Maud de Braose. She married John de Brompton. She would have been of the right generation to support Eleanor. It is also possible that one of Matilda's grandmothers, aunts or older cousins in the Saint-Valery family, also called Maud, may have fulfilled this role.

## Two Welsh Legends
The malevolence felt amongst the Welsh against Matilda is reflected in the stories of her being a witch. They are illustrated by two tales that occur in folklore:

LEGEND ONE
This involves a tale similar to that of William Tell, who had to shoot an apple off his son's head. The Welsh prince Madog was also required to do this after his lands were confiscated. He did so successfully, but that night Madog returned with his cousin Black Judge. They caught and hanged Matilda and her son before

escaping to the Cothi Valley.[25] The origin of this story is lost and not borne out in any way by the facts as we know them.

CONCLUSION

This legend shows the level of hatred felt by the Welsh for Matilda, and perhaps even sorrow and regret that they were not responsible for her death.

LEGEND TWO

A second story is more of a myth, not directly attributed to Matilda, but clearly arises in the Anglo-Norman period when Matilda was prominent in Hay. It tells the tale of an old crone who races across the sky with hounds, hunting for lost souls.[26] She is called 'Mallt y Nos', 'Night Mallt' or 'Matilda of the Night'. Perhaps the name is not coincidental, as a variation tells of a Norman hunting woman. When she is rebuked for her love of hunting, she replies that she would prefer to hunt than go to heaven. As a result, on stormy nights, she is condemned to travel through the air with the Hounds of Hell.[27]

CONCLUSION

Matilda's reputation meant that her name was appended to these stories because she was felt to have displayed unladylike qualities in her aggressive support of her husband.

In addition to the legends about Matilda, one exists relating to her husband William. This is recorded in *Brut-y-Tywysogion*, *The Chronicles of the Princes*, although inevitably there are a number of versions.[28]

LEGEND ABOUT WILLIAM

*The abduction of a Welsh Lady.* Despite his reputation, there does not seem to have been much interest in generating any legends or malevolent stories about William. The one that does exist appears in two versions, neither of which are complimentary.

William and his men were out hawking on the hills in Maelienydd (north Radnorshire), a few miles from Hay, when they came upon a beautiful lady and her attendants at Llan Bwch-llyn pool. She was the daughter of the owner of The Skreen, a mansion at the nearby village of Erwood. William abducted them all to Elfael.

The girl was from the Welsh royal line and her relatives hunted for her everywhere, but all the time suspected Norman knights had taken her to Painscastle. They watched and saw a light in the window of the castle tower, and a locket owned by the lady. They appealed to Prince Rhys ap Gruffydd for help but, when approached, William denied any knowledge of the girl. He claimed he had been slandered. Rhys did not believe William and besieged the castle, forcing William to come to terms and release her.

In the other version of the legend there is a giant 'Norman King' landlord (almost certainly an allusion to William). He abducts the girl, a Miss Phillips, when she is found with her lover Arthur at Llan Bwch-llyn pool. While waiting for help to arrive, a woman from Painscastle assists the girl to escape, dressed as a soldier. Her lover fails to recognise her and shoots her dead. Arthur then attacks and kills the giant, before a battle between the Norman forces of Hay and Clifford castles, and the Welsh from Old Radnor and Cefn y Blaen. Needless to say, the Welsh are triumphant.[29]

BASIS FOR THE LEGEND

It is recorded that Rhys attacked Painscastle, forcing William to come to terms in 1196, two years before the better-known siege of Painscastle by Gwenwynwyn. There is no record of a lady in the tower on this occasion but another incident involving a Rhys, a lady and a tower happened years later. Rhys ap Maredudd captured one of the royal castles of Edward I and left his wife there while he continued on to attack the English. Rhys was driven back and only narrowly managed to rescue his wife from the castle, probably by signalling with a light at a window in a tower.

CONCLUSION

A mixture of fact and fiction has been used by the Welsh to blacken the name of one of the most hated Anglo-Normans and show the Welsh in a better light. It is perhaps incidental that the current building called The Skreen has parts dating to the sixteenth century. Perhaps there was an earlier building of the same name on the site.

∼

## APPENDIX 1: THE LITERARY HERITAGE OF MATILDA

Matilda may have been a strong, powerful woman but she lived at a time when women had few rights. Historically, they have often been overlooked, unless for example they held vast estates, or bore children who eventually came to the throne or were royal consorts. Matilda did none of these things, and yet despite this she has achieved a level of immortality.

Non-fiction

Most members of the monarchy have numerous biographies written about them and John is no exception. He was the first royal to compile extensive, accurate administrative records that have survived. These, together with official state papers, mean there is plenty of material for royal biographers.

Militarily, the vast Angevin empire left by Henry II was largely lost by John. This was despite the large amount of campaigning he did. A catalyst for many of his woes was Arthur's death. John's pursuit of the de Braoses led to his armies going into Wales, Scotland and Ireland. All this is great fodder for the military historian. John was also generally acknowledged to have been an unpleasant man. His personal qualities create opportunities to explore instances of his intrigues and deceit. These are popular with authors and readers alike. In John's case, examples of his villainy include the death of Arthur of Brittany, the downfall of William and the tragic manner of Matilda's death.

These events are linked together through William's custody of Arthur, and Matilda's reference to Arthur's death in her exchange with John's messengers. This adds depth to almost any account of John's life. As a consequence, there are a number of biographies and a considerable body of factual history about John, which include reference to Matilda.

## Historical Fiction

The established historical facts provide sufficient material for the writers of historical fiction to create intriguing story-lines. Strong characters in turbulent times with just enough facts to provide an understanding of events, allow opportunities for wide interpretation. Villainous King John, innocent Arthur, ruthless undiplomatic but loyal warrior William, and arrogant, tragic Matilda give ample scope for novelists to weave their tales.

## Matilda de Braose

A number of novels make reference to Matilda and portray key events in her life to a greater or lesser extent.

1. Chadwick, Elizabeth, *The Scarlet Lion* (William Marshal, 2007) and *To Defy a King* (Sphere, 2011).
A noted historian and speaker on medieval subjects, Chadwick uses the established facts as the basis for her stories. These books demonstrate why the author has been described as one of the best historical novelists of the age.

2. Davies, Elizabeth, *The Spirit Guide* (Publishing Platform, 2014)
Although making no attempt to portray historical events in themselves, this uses Matilda and Hay Castle to frame a story about the supernatural, a medieval castle and perhaps Matilda's reputation as a witch.

3. Erskine, Barbara, *The Lady of Hay* (Harper, 2011)
This international best-selling novel has Matilda at the heart of the story. All the established historical facts are accurately portrayed in a time-travelling tale linking events to modern times.

4. Kaufman, Pamela, *The Prince of Poison* (Broadway Books, 2006)
A fictional character is used to frame a story which includes events in Matilda's life and many of those relating to King John.

5. Penman, Sharon, *Here Be Dragons* (Penguin, 1991)
An author whose novels are so realistic, and based on known facts, that they are recommended as background reading by at least one lecturer on medieval Welsh history.[1]

6. Plaidy, Jean, *The Prince of Darkness* (Arrow, 2007)
In the style of a traditional, romantic novel involving Matilda, this story captures the avaricious nature of King John, and how many of his actions were consequent on the circumstances he found himself in.

William III de Braose
Despite his fierce reputation as 'The Ogre of Abergavenny', William has been neglected as the subject of medieval warrior tales, with one notable exception:

Scott, Sir Walter, *The Betrothed*, (Tales of the Crusaders, 1825)
Although this novel was initially well received, later reviewers have concluded that perhaps it is not one of Scott's best.

Maud de Braose
Norton, Fran, *The Twisted Legacy of Maud de Braose Lady of Wigmore Castle* (YouCaxton Publications, 2016)
This novel is not about Matilda but concerns the daughter of her grandson William v, who was described as sharing Matilda's strong character traits. The book is set in the Marcher lands north of Hay. The author is a member of the Mortimer History Society and she has built her fictional story around the known historical facts of the de Braose and Mortimer families.

GATE OF HAY CASTLE.

This apparently romanticised image of the ruins of Hay Castle is actually not far from the reality of its condition in the nineteenth century. It illustrates the state into which the castle had fallen in recent centuries, and why the Hay Castle Trust was set up to restore the site and ensure its survival for future generations

Matilda will forever be associated with Hay Castle, her home and base for many years. She is credited with building the large stone gateway and curtain walls, in order to improve the rudimentary defences presumed to have existed around the original square stone keep that overlooks the present market square.

The castle was attacked and 'destroyed' by King John in 1216 and Llywelyn ab Iorwerth in 1230, but from then on it ceased to be militarily significant. It changed hands a number of times but these were mostly peaceful transfers and no large-scale battles are known to have occurred. Various accounts show that it was strengthened in the early 1400s against the threat of Owen Glyn Dŵr but he did not attack the castle as far as is known. The names of the 20 archers sent from the garrison to the Battle of Agincourt in 1415 are recorded at Brecon Cathedral.

The castle finally became redundant in the time of Henry VIII when the Acts of Union in 1535 and 1543 formally united England and Wales. Parts of the castle were demolished, and changes were made to the keep in the 1570s when the first mansion was built on the site. It was only a few decades later, in around 1630, that this building was completely remodelled and incorporated into the fine Jacobean mansion that has dominated the town ever since.

The mansion was occupied by a variety of owners and tenants for 200 years before being bought by Joseph Bailey, the prominent South Wales ironmaster. His nephew, Archdeacon William Latham Bevan, vicar of Hay, occupied it for over 50 years in the second half of the nineteenth century. In 1870, Francis Kilvert's diaries record his participation in archery on the lawns with Bevan's daughters. The well-known architect William

Douglas Caröe refurbished the mansion in 1910 during the occupancy of dowager Lady Mary Glanusk, who lived there between 1906 and 1936. An article in the *Country Life* of August 1914 shows that it was one of the most impressive mansions of its type in the country.

Significant visitors at this time included Prince Frederick Duleep Singh in 1913. 'Prince Freddy' was the son of the last Maharaja of the Sikh Empire, and his sister was a famous suffragette, Princess Sonia Duleep Singh. On 23 April 1914 Lieutenant Sir Robert S.S. Baden-Powell visited and fished for salmon in the Hay Castle waters down on the River Wye.

Since then, the castle's fortunes have declined. The castle site remained in private ownership, and there were disastrous fires in 1939 and 1977. Despite repairs, the ravages of time and neglect meant the buildings were in a poor state and required extensive stabilisation and restoration in order to preserve them.

The Hay Castle Trust was formed in 2011, to preserve the remaining castle and mansion for future generations. With £4.45 million of Heritage Lottery Funding and generous donations from a number of trusts, an extensive refurbishment and improvement programme was initiated in 2019. These works have entailed the renovation and stabilisation of the house and original castle; the restoration of the gatehouse and castle gates (one dating from around 1340, the other from around 1640); the provision of an observation deck to the keep, to provide extensive views across the Wye Valley and into Radnorshire; the opening of the buildings and grounds to the public; and the addition of a café, an area for meetings, an education centre for all ages and a fine exhibition gallery.

Although there is further work to do, including to the curtain wall, it is now possible to walk through the gates and into the keep, in the footsteps of Matilda, Lady of Hay.

# NOTES AND REFERENCES

INTRODUCTION

1   Thorpe, Lewis, trans., *Gerald of Wales: The Journey through Wales and The Description of Wales*, Penguin Books (London, 1978).
2   Gough-Cooper, Henry, ed., *The Cottonian Chronicle: Annales Cambriae*, The C Text from London, British Library, Cotton MS Domitian A. i, ff.138r–155r, http://croniclau.bangor.ac.uk/documents/AC_A_first_edition.pdf
3   Jones, Thomas, ed. and trans., *Brut y Tywysogyon or the Chronicle of the Princes: Red Book of Hergest Version*, University of Wales Press (Cardiff, 1955).
4   Charles-Edwards, T.M., *The Welsh Laws*, Writers of Wales Series, University of Wales Press (Cardiff, 1989).
5   Davies, R.R., 'The Laws of the March', *The Welsh History Review*, Vol. 5, University of Wales Press, National Library of Wales (Cardiff, 1971), 1–30.
6   Ibid.

CHAPTER ONE

1   Lewis, Christopher Lloyd, ed., Clay, Charles Travis and Douglas, David C., *The Origins of Some Anglo-Norman Families*, The Harleian Society, Reprinted by Genealogical Publishing Company (Leeds, 1975).
2   See Chapter 3.
3   Untitled English Nobility. This is a very extensive list: http://fmg.ac/Projects/MedLands/ENGLISHNOBILITYMEDIEVAL3.htm#
4   Luard, Henry Richards, ed., *Annales Monastici: Annales prioratus de Dunstaplia (AD 1–1297), Annales monasterii de Bermundesia (AD 1042–1432)*, Vols. I and II (1864).
5   Hardy, T. D., ed., *Rotuli Chartarum*, Royal Commission (London, 1837).
6   Boulter, Matthew, *The Career of William III de Briouze in the Reign of King John: Land, Power and Social Ties*. MA Sheffield University at William de Briouze. Rtf.
7   Murphy, Paul, *Destination Hay: A Guide to the Independent Kingdom of Hay-on-Wye*, Great Little Destination Guides (2018).
8   See Chapter 3.
9   *Rotuli Litterarum Patentium*, I, 4, 7, 16b, 18b, 19b, 24b, in McLynn, Frank, *Lionheart and Lackland*, Jonathan Cape (2006).
10  Holt, J.C., *The Northerners: A Study in the Reign of King John*, Oxford (1961).
11  Painter, Sidney, *The Reign of King John*, John Hopkins Press (Baltimore, 1949).
12  Pipe Roll of 1207 p. 38.
13  Reoch, Ernest, *The St. Valery Story*, Highland Press (Michigan, 1965).
14  Michel, Francisque, ed., Nicholson, Dr Helen, trans., *L'Histoire des Ducs de Normandie et des Rois d'Angleterre* (Paris, 1840).

15  Mount, Toni, *The Medieval Housewife and other women of the Middle Ages*, Amberley Publishing (Stroud, 2014).

16  Blackstone, Sir William, *Commentaries on the Laws of England (1765–1769)*, Clarendon Press (Oxford, 2005) https://lonang.com/library.

17  Stevens, M.F., 'Women and the Law in the Age of Magna Carta', Lecture at the Mortimer History Society spring conference (2015).

18  Mount, Toni, *The Medieval Housewife and other women of the Middle Ages*, Amberley Publishing (Stroud, 2014).

19  Medieval lingerie from Lengberg Castle, East-Tyrol, Research project ABT, https://www.uibk.ac.at/urgeschichte/projekte_forschung/textilien-lengberg/mittelalterliche-unterwaesche/index.html.en.

20  Anonymous of Bethune, *Contemporary Chronicles: The Contest over the Past* (*c.*1220), University of California Press.

21  See Chapter 4.

22  Thorpe, Lewis, trans., *Gerald of Wales: The Journey through Wales and The Description of Wales*, Penguin Books (London, 1978).

23  Butler, H.E., trans., *De rebus a se gestis: The Autobiography of Giraldus Cambrensis*, Jonathan Cape (London, 1937).

24  Ibid.

25  Remfry, P.M. *The Castles and History of Radnorshire*, Castle Studies Research and Publishing (2008).

26  Clare, Horatio, *Brecon Beacons Myths and Legends*, Graffeg (Llanelli, 2017).

27  Michel, Francisque, ed., *L'Histoire de ducs de Normandie et des Rois d'Angleterre* (Paris, 1840).

28  Camden, William (Holland, Philemon, trans.), *"The Author to the Reader". Britain, or a Chorographical Description of the most flourishing Kingdoms, England, Scotland, and Ireland, and the Islands adjoyning, out of the depth of Antiquitie*, (London, 1610).

29  Anonymous of Bethune, *Contemporary Chronicles: The Contest over the Past* (*c.*1220), University of California Press.


CHAPTER TWO

1   Anonymous of Bethune in Michel, Francisque, ed., Nicholson, Dr Helen, trans., *L'Histoire des Ducs de Normandie et des Rois d'Angleterre* (Paris, 1840).

2   PRO ref, E164/12; Ref. L.B. fol. 419, *Penes Camerar: Scaccar*, recorded in Rymer's *Foedera*, vol. 1, 52.

3   Powel, David, *The Historie of Cambria, Now called Wales: A Part of the Most Famous Yland of Brystaine, Written in the Brytish Language Aboue Two Hundreth Yeares Past: Translated into English by H. Lhoyd Gentleman: Corrected, Augmented, and Continued out of Records and Best Approoued Authors* (London, 1584) 248.

4   Hume, Philip, *On the Trail of the Mortimers*, Logaston Press (Almeley, 2016).

5   Michel, Francisque, ed., *L'Histoire de ducs de Normandie et des Rois d'Angleterre*, (Paris, 1840).

6   National library of Wales MS 13144A – Bardism, miscellanea, https://archives.library.wales/index.php/bardism-miscellanea

7   Williams, Jonathan, *A General History of the County of Radnor*, Davies and Son (Hereford, 1905).

8   Royal Commission for Ancient Historic Monuments of Wales.

9    Robinson, C.J., *A History of the Mansions and Manors of Herefordshire*, Logaston Press (Almeley, 2001).

10   Fairs, Geoffrey, *A History of The Hay*, Phillimore (Chichester, 1972).

11   Round, Anc. Charters p. 8 in Hearne, Thomas, ed., *The Itinerary of John Leland the Antiquary*, 2nd edition, vol. 6 (1744–45).

12   Fairs, Geoffrey, *The History of the Hay*, Phillimore (Chichester, 1972).

13   Phillips, T.P. *The Brecknockshire Border*, Talgarth (D.J. Morgan, 1926) 51.

CHAPTER THREE

1    Holt, J.C., 'King John and Arthur of Brittany', *Nottinghamshire Medieval Studies*, 44 (2000) 9.

2    Hindley, Geoffrey, *The Book of Magna Carta*, Constable (London, 1990).

3    Crouch, David, *William Marshal*, Routledge (2016).

4    Holden, A.J., Gregory, S. and Crouch, D. eds. *The History of William Marshal*. Anglo-Norman Text Society, occasional publications nos. 4–6 (2002–6).

5    Church, Stephen, *King John: England, Magna Carta and the making of a Tyrant*, Macmillan (London, 2015).

6    Carpenter, David, *Magna Carta*, Penguin (London, 2015).

7    Laurd, H.R., *Annales Monasticum*. Vol. 1 (1869).

8    Church, Stephen, *King John: England, Magna Carta and the making of a Tyrant*, Macmillan (London, 2015).

9    Holt, J.C., 'King John and Arthur of Brittany', *Nottinghamshire Medieval Studies*, 44 (2000) 82–103.

10   *Oxford Dictionary of National Biography* (2004) http://www.oxforddnb.com/.

11   Delaborde, H.F., ed., *Oeuvres de Rigord et Guillaume le Breton* (Paris, 1885).

12   Turner, Ralph V., *King John*, History Press (Cheltenham, 2015) 253.

13   Carpenter, D., *The Struggle for Mastery: Britain 1066–1284*, Penguin (London, 2003).

14   Crouch, David, *William Marshal: Court, Career and Chivalry in the Angevine Empire, 1147–1219* (London, 1990) 91, 94, 99.

15   Holden, A.J., Gregory, S. and Crouch, D. eds. and translators, *The History of William Marshal*, Anglo Norman Text Society, Birkbeck College (2003).

16   Asbridge, Thomas, *The Greatest Knight*, Simon and Schuster (London, 2015).

17   Hardy, ed. *Rotuli Chartarum*.

18   Giles, J.A. trans., *Roger of Wendover's Flowers of History* (1849).

19   *The Annals of Margam Abbey 1066–1232*.

20   *Close Roll*, 25 January 1206.

21   Murphy, Paul, *Destination Hay: A Guide to the Independent Kingdom of Hay-on-Wye*, Great Little Destination Guides (2018).

22   Starkey, D., *Magna Carta: The True Story Behind the Charter*, Hodder (London, 2015).

23   PRO ref. E164/12; Ref. L.B. fol. 419. *Penes Camerar. Scaccar*, Recorded in Rhymers's Foedera, Vol. 1, 52.

24   Crouch, D., 'The Complaint of King John against William de Briouze', in Loengard, J. S., ed., *Magna Carta and the England of King John*, Woodbridge (2010).

25   Veach, C., 'King John and Royal Control in Ireland: Why William de Briouze had to be Destroyed', *English Historical Review*, 129 (2014) 1053–63.

26   Duffy, Sean, 'King John's Expedition to Ireland in 1210: the Evidence Reconsidered', *Irish Historical Studies*, 30 (1996) 1–24.

27   Veach, C., 'King John and Royal Control in Ireland: Why William de Briouze had to be Destroyed', *English Historical Review*, 129 (2014) 1053–63.

28  Morris, Marc, *King John: Treachery, Tyranny and the Road to Magna Carta*, Windmill Books (London, 2015).
29  *William of Newburgh*, I, p.521.
30  Carpenter, D., *The Struggle for Mastery: Britain 1066–1284*, Penguin (London, 2003).
31  Ibid.
32  Michel, Francisque, ed., Nicholson, Dr Helen, trans., *L'Histoire des Ducs de Normandie et des Rois d'Angleterre* (Paris, 1840).
33  Norgate, Kate, *John Lackland*, Forgotten Books (2017).
34  Greaves, Ronald, 'The Galloway lands in Ulster', in *The Transactions of the Dumfriesshire and Galloway Natural History and Antiquarian Society*, Vol. 36 (1957–8) 115–22.
35  Stevenson, J., *Radolphi de Coggeshall, Chronicon Anglicanum*, Rolls series (1875).
36  Howes, Russell, 'Magna Carta and Two Sheriffs of Gloucestershire', *Glevensis*, 38, Gloucestershire and District Archaeological Group (2005). http://www.gadarg.org.uk/essays/e012.htm
37  Fitzgerald, Waverly, *School of the Seasons*, https://www.schooloftheseasons.com/
38  Anonymous of Bethune, *Contemporary Chronicles: The Contest over the Past* (*c.*1220), University of California Press.
39  Painter, Sidney, *The Reign of King John*, John Hopkins Press (Baltimore, 1966).

CHAPTER FOUR
1   British Library, *The Cotton MS Julius D*, x.
2   Lloyd, John Edward, *A History of Wales from the earliest times to the Edwardian Conquest*, Longmans, Green & Co. (1911).
3   British Library, *The Cotton MS Julius D*, x.
4   *Pipe Roll* 5 John 28 March, Public Record Office (1205).
5   British Library, *The Cotton MS Julius D*, x.
6   Crawley-Boevey, Arthur William, *The Cartulary and Historical Notes of the Cistercian Abbey of Flaxley*, William Pollard (Exeter, 1887) 134.
7   Remfry, P.M., *The Castles and History of Radnorshire*, Castle Studies Research and Publishing (2008).
8   Morgan, G.E.F. 'The Vanished tombs of Brecknock Cathedral', *Archaeologia Cambrensis* 80 (1925) 257–724. http://www.monasticwales.org/source/396.
9   Barrow, J.S., ed., *Fasti Ecclesiae Anglicanae 1066–1300*: Volume 8, Hereford, Institute of Historical Research (London, 2002).
10  *Curia Regis Rolls V*, 152.
11  *Leland's Itineraries V*, 163.
12  Fisher, Alfred Hugh, *Bell's Cathedrals: The Cathedral Church of Hereford, A Description Of Its Fabric And A Brief History Of The Episcopal See*, Lector House (2019).
13  Holden, Brock, 'King John, the Braoses, and the Celtic Fringe 1207–1216', in *Albion: Journal of British Studies* (2001).
14  Salzman L.F., ed., *The Victoria History of the County of Oxford* (London, 1907) 75.
15  Amt, Emily, 'The Latin Cartulary of Godstow Abbey', *Records of Social and Economic History* Vol. 52, British Academy (Oxford, 2014).
16  Labarge, M.W., 'Three Medieval Widows and Second Careers', in *Aging and the Aged in Medieval Europe*, ed., Sheehan, M.M. (Toronto, 1997) 159–72.
17  Pearson, Hilary, 'The Life and Times of Annora' (Papers Delivered at Conference in Iffley on 7th July 2018) https://iffleychurch.org.uk.

18  Labarge, M.W., *A Medieval Miscellany*, McGill-Queen's University Press (1997).
19  Powicke, F.M. 'Loretta, Countess of Leicester', in Edwards, J.G. et al., eds., *Historical Essays in Honour of James Tait* (Manchester, 1933) 247–274.
20  Welcome to St Mary's Iffley https://iffleychurch.org.uk/living-stones/annora/
21  Nicholson, H., 'Margaret de Lacy and the Hospital of St John at Aconbury Herefordshire', *The Journal of Ecclesiastical History*, 50(4) (1999) 629–651.
22  Innes-Parker, Catherine, 'Medieval Widowhood and Textural Guidance: the Corpus Revisions of Ancrene Wisse and the de Braose Anchoresses', *Florilegium*, Vol. 28 (2011) 95–124.

CHAPTER FIVE

1  Vincent, Nicholas, *Magna Carta: A Very Short Introduction*, Oxford University Press (Oxford, 2012) 59–60.
2  British Library, *Magna Carta Collection* https://www.bl.uk.
3  Carpenter, David, *Magna Carta*, Penguin Classics (London, 2015).
4  Ibid.
5  Paris, Luard H.R. ed., *Matthaei Parisiensis, monachi Santi Monastici*, Vol. 2 of Rolls Series (London, 1872–83).
6  Jones, Dan, *The Plantagenets: the Kings who Made England*, William Collins (London, 2012).
7  Holden, Brock, 'King John, the Braoses and the Celtic Fringe 1207–1216', *Albion: Journal of British Studies* (2001).
8  See Chapter 3.
9  Bailey, Mabel, *The Myths and Legends of Brecknockshire* (1909).
10  Timmins, Henry T., *Nooks and Corners in Herefordshire* (London, 1892) 95.
11  Ibid.
12  Jones, Theophilus, *History of Brecknock*, Blissett, Davis and Co. (Brecknock, 1909).
13  Hartland, E., 'Notes on a Radnorshire Cross', *Archaelogia Cambrensis*, 4 ser. IV (1873) 325.
14  Ibid.
15  Jones, Theophilus, *History of Brecknock*, Blissett, Davis and Co. (Brecknock, 1909).
16  Thorpe, Lewis, trans., *Gerald of Wales: The Journey through Wales and The Description of Wales*, Penguin Books (London, 1978).
17  Mortimer, I., *The Time Traveller's Guide to Medieval England*, Vintage Books (2009).
18  Williams, Jonathan, *A General History of the County of Radnor*, Davies and Son (Hereford, 1905) 201.
19  Williams, J., 'The History of Radnorshire', *Archaelogia Cambrensis*, 3 ser. I (1858) 533.
20  Williams, Jonathan, *A General History of the County of Radnor*, Davies and Son (Hereford, 1905).
21  Gill, M.A.V., *The Parish Churches of the Wye Valley* (2010).
22  Somerset, Anne, *Ladies in Waiting*, Phoenix (2005).
23  Meade, Marion, *Eleanor of Aquitaine*, Orion Books (London, 1977).
24  Ibid.
25  Peniarth MSS 131, in Evan, J.G., *Report on Manuscripts in the Welsh Language*, Vol. 1 (London, 1898–1910) 819.
26  Trevelyan, Marie, *Folk-lore and folk stories of Wales*, Elliott Stock (London, 1909). https://archive.org/details/afl2317.0001.001.umich.edu.
27  Beare, B., *Wales: Myths and Legends* (Bristol, 1958).

28    Baring-Gould, Sabine, *A Book of South Wales* (1905)
      https://archive.org/stream/abooksouthwales 7.01.18
29    Kilvert, F., *Kilvert's Diary 1870–1879*, in Plomer, W., ed., Vintage Books (London,
      2013) 28 March 1870.

APPENDIX 1

1    Dr John R. Kenyon, late of the National Library of Wales.

An engraving showing Matilda's new gateway into the castle, built next to
the keep. Her new castle walls can be seen just to the left

## SOURCES

Details of the principal characters can be found in *The Oxford Dictionary of National Biography* (2004) http://www.oxforddnb.com/

Primary Sources

Cotton Manuscripts, multiple folios – *de Braose*, Julius D., *28r-30r; Annals of Tewkesbury*. Cleopatra A, vii 7–103; *The Annals of Waverly*, Vespasian A xvi, British Library.

Fowler, C.T., *Curia Regis Rolls*, (Kings Court Rolls), Public Record Office (London, 1922–27).

Gerald of Wales, archdeacon of Brecknock, provides the main contemporary account of Matilda and William. There are 3 versions of his writings starting with his account of *The Itinerary of Archbishop Baldwin through Wales* in 1188, recruiting for the Third Crusade. Project Gutenberg: http://www.gutenberg.org/files/1148/1148-0.txt

Luard, Henry Richards, ed., 'Annals of Margam' in *Annales Monastic, recte Margam 1, 36* (1864, reprint 1965).

Ralph of Coggeshall *Radulphi de Coggeshall Chronicon Anglicanum*. Rolls series No 66.

Riley, H.T. ed., *The Annals of Roger De Hoveden (1853)*.

Roger of Newburgh in Walsh, P.G. and Kennedy, M.J. ed., and trans., *The History of English Affairs* (2007).

Roger of Wendover, *Flores Historiarum* (1235).

St Valery Connection

Descendants of Bernard de St Valery:
  https://www.ourfamtree.org/descend.php/Bernard-de-St-Valery/4504
St Valery Family: http://helenesgenes.com/SaintValery.html
Descendants of Guilbert de St Valery:
  http://washington.ancestryregister.com/ST._VALERY00006.htm.
An important source for what we know about Matilda's early life is the thirteenth-century *Histoire des Ducs de Normandie et des Rois d'Angleterre*. This appears to have been written by someone who knew many of the individuals named. For a translation of some of this see Dr Helen Nicholson's website: http://booksrus.me.uk/hn/indexwomen.html.
David Nash Ford's Royal Berkshire History,
  http://www.berkshirehistory.com/bios/msrvalery.html

De Braose Family History

There are numerous references to the de Braose family online, with a number of family trees of varying size and complexity. Details on many of the websites agree, but there are also significant differences, and care is needed in the interpretation of these sources.

The following provide a basis:

The Barons de Braose: http://douglyn.co.uk/BraoseWeb/frames.html

David Nash Ford's Royal Berkshire History:
  http://www.berkshirehistory.com/bios/msrvalery.html

Wiki Tree: https://www.wikitree.com/genealogy/Braose-Descendants-2

RootsWeb: http://sites.rootsweb.com/~cousin/html/p384.htm#i6760

Wikipedia: https://en.wikipedia.org/wiki/House_of_Braose

Loretta as an anchoress: https://iffleychurch.org.uk/1the-original-plan-of-the-church/08-the-tower-and-the-south-wall/annora/

Cawley, Charles. Medieval Lands website. Foundation for Medieval Genealogy.

Geni https://www.geni.com/.

The Society for Medieval Military History. This site has numerous articles on many aspects of medieval history: http://deremilitari.org/articles/

Untitled English Nobility. This is a very extensive list:
  http://fmg.ac/Projects/MedLands/ENGLISHNOBILITYMEDIEVAL3.htm#_Toc389040796.

For details of the downfall of the de Braoses, see references: Holden, B.

Details of the de Braose Sussex estates, Steyning Museum:
  http://steyningmuseum.org.uk/historypage.htm.

For the most detailed account of William's estates, reference needs to be made to the Pipe Rolls, Book of Fees and the Red Book of the Exchequer, and numerous royal charters. The *curia regia* rolls (detailing litigation he was involved in) also refer to his estates.

King John

Church, Stephen, *King John: England, Magna Carta and the making of a Tyrant*, Macmillan, (London, 2015).

Jones, Dan, *The Plantagenets: The Kings who made England*, William Collins (London, 2013).

Morris, Marc, *King John: Treachery, Tyranny and the Road to Magna Carta*, Windmill Books, (London, 2015).

Death of Arthur

Ralph of Coggeshall describes the incarceration at Falaise.

*The Annals of Margam Abbey 1066–1232* gives a full account.

*Philippide* was a poem written by William the Breton, King Philip's chaplain. Book IV of the poem was written before 1214 and gives a similar but partially different account, indicating it was independent to the Annals of Margam.

Wechelen, the Hermit of Llowes

Davis, Revd D.S., 'Wechelen: The Hermit of Llowes' in the *Transactions of the Radnorshire Society*, Vol. 2 (1932) 7–8, cites as his sources *The Book of Llan Dav*, Newells' *History of the Welsh Church*, Brewer's *Geraldi Cambrensis* Opera, Henry Owen's *Gerald the Welshman*, and Dr J.E. Lloyd's *History of Wales* (Leopold Classic Library, 2016).

# BIBLIOGRAPHY

Birch, Walter de Gray, *A History of Margam Abbey* (account written in the thirteenth century), Wentworth Press (2016).

Boulter, Matthew, *The Career of William III de Briouze in the Reign of King John: Land, Power and Social Ties* (Undated).

Butler, H.E., trans. *De rebus a se gestis: The Autobiography of Giraldus Cambrensis*, Jonathan Cape (1937).

Carpenter, David, *Magna Carta*, Penguin (2015).

Church, Stephen, *King John: England, Magna Carta and the making of a Tyrant*, Macmillan (London, 2015).

Clare, Horatio, *Brecon Beacons Myths and Legends*, Graffeg (Llanelli, 2017).

Crouch, D., 'The Complaint of King John against William de Briouze', in Loengard, J.S. ed. *Magna Carta and the England of King John*, Woodbridge (2010).

Danziger, Danny and Gillingham, *John: 1215 The Year of the Magna Carta*, Hodder and Stoughton (London, 2003).

Davis, Rev. D. Stedman, 'Wechelen, The Hermit of Llowes', in *Radnorshire Society Transactions* Vol 2, (1932) 7–8.

Duffy, Sean, 'King John's expedition to Ireland, 1210: The evidence reconsidered', in *Irish Historical Studies*, Vol. 30 (1996) 117.

Dugdale, William, *Dugdales Monasticon VI, Llanthony Abbey, Gloucestershire II, Fundatorum Progenies* (1655–73) 134.

Fairs, Geoffrey, *A History of The Hay*, Chichester, Phillimore (1972).

Gildas Research, *The Inventory of Historic Battlefields in Wales*, Royal Commission on the Historic Monuments in Wales (2013). http://battlefields.rcahmw.gov.uk

Giles, A.J., trans., *Roger of Wendover's Flowers of History*, Classic reprint, Forgotten Books (2018).

Gill, M.A.V., 'Scheduled Ancient Monument R100 (SO 192417): The Cross-Slab in St Meilig's Church, Llowes' in the *Transactions of the Radnorshire Society*, Vol. LXXI (2001) 19–55.

Gillingham, John, 'Anonymous of Bethune, King John and the Magna Carta' in Loengard, J.S., *Magna Carta and the England of King John*, Boydell and Brewer (2010).

Hartland, E., 'Notes on a Radnorshire Cross', *Archaeologia Cambrensis*, 4 ser IV (1873) 325.

Holden, Brock, 'King John, the Braoses, and the Celtic Fringe 1207–1216', in *Albion: Journal of British Studies* (2001).

Holt, J.C., 'King John and Arthur of Brittany', *Nottinghamshire Medieval Studies* (2000) 44.

Innes-Parker, Christina, 'The Recluse and its Reader: Some Observations on a Lollard interpolated version of the Ancrene Wisse', in *A Companion to the Ancrene Wisse*, Wada, Yoko, ed. (2003).

Innes-Parker, Catherine, 'Medieval Widowhood and Textural Guidance: The Corpus Revisions of Ancrene Wisse and the de Braose Anchoresses', *Florilegium*, vol.28 (2011) 95–124.

Jones, Dan, *Magna Carta: The Making and Legacy of the Great Charter*, Head of Zeus (2014).

— *The Plantagenets: the Kings who Made England*, William Collins (2012).

— *Realm Divided*, London, Head of Zeus (2015).

Jones, Thomas, ed., *Brut y Tywysogyon: Peniarth MS. 20 Version*, University of Wales Press (1952).

Kilvert, F., *Kilverts Diary 1870 – 1879*, Plomer, W., ed., Vintage Books (London, 2013).

Lewis, Christopher Lloyd; Travis Clay, Charles and Douglas, David Charles, *The Origins of Some Anglo-Norman Families*, The Harleian Society, reprinted by the Genealogical Publishing Company (Leeds, 1975).

Matthew, H.C.G. and Harrison, B., *The Oxford Dictionary of National Biography*, 60 vols. Oxford University Press (2004). http://oxforddnb.com

Michel, Francisque, ed., *Nicholson, Dr Helen, trans., Histoire des Ducs de Normandie et des Rois d'Angleterre* (Paris, 1840). http://booksrus.me.uk/hn/indexwomen.html

Morris, Marc, *King John: Treachery, Tyranny and the Road to Magna Carta*, Windmill Books (London, 2015).

Nicholls, Alan J., *The Lords of Hay*, Lulu (2015).

Nicholson, H., 'Margaret de Lacy and the Hospital of St John at Aconbury Herefordshire', in *The Journal of Ecclesiastical History*, 50(4) (1999) 629–51.

Painter, Sidney, *The Reign of King John*, John Hopkins Press (Baltimore, 1966).

Powicke F.M., 'King John and Arthur of Brittany' in *The English Historical Review*, Oxford University Press. Vol. 24, No. 96 (1909) 659–74.

Powicke, F.M., 'Loretta, countess of Leicester' in *Historical Essays presented to James Tait*, eds., Edwards, J.G., Galbraith, V.H. and Jacob, E.F. (Manchester, 1933).

Rymer, Thomas, PRO ref. E164/12; Ref. L.B. fol. 419. *Penes Camerar. Scaccar*, Recorded in *Rymers's Foedera*. Vol 1 (London, 1816) 52.

Reoch, Ernest, *The St. Valery Story*, Highland Printers (Michigan, 1965).

Thorpe, Lewis., trans. *Gerald of Wales: The Journey through Wales and The Description of Wales*, Penguin Books (London, 1978).

Untitled English Nobility. English Lords A-C. This is a very extensive list: http://fmg.ac/Projects/MedLands/ENGLISHNOBILITYMEDIEVAL3.htm#_Toc389040796

Veach, C., 'King John and Royal Control in Ireland: Why William de Briouze had to be Destroyed' in *English Historical Review*, 129 (2014).

Welcome to St Mary's Iffley: https://iffleychurch.org.uk/living-stones/annora/

Williams, Jonathan, *A General History of the County of Radnor*, Davies and Son (Hereford, 1905).

# INDEX